DAILY
THE BLESS

Eucharistic
Gems

DONALD H. CALLOWAY, MIC

Available from:
Marian Helpers Center
Stockbridge, MA 01263

Prayerline: 1-800-804-3823
Orderline: 1-800-462-7426
Websites: fathercalloway.com
Marian.org

Publication Date:
February 1, 2023

Imprimi Potest:
Very Rev. Chris Alar, MIC
Provincial Superior
The Blessed Virgin Mary, Mother of Mercy Province
January 1, 2023
Solemnity of Mary, Mother of God

Nihil Obstat:
Robert A. Stackpole, STD
Censor Deputatus
January 1, 2023

ISBN: 978-1-59614-590-0
Library of Congress Control Number: 2023902295

Printed in the United States of America

If souls understood what treasure they possess in the divine Eucharist, it would be necessary to protect tabernacles with impregnable ramparts; because in the delirium of a holy and devouring hunger, they would go themselves to feed on the Manna of the Seraphim. Churches, at night as in daytime, would overflow with worshipers wasting away with love for the august prisoner.

– BLESSED DINA BÉLANGER

INTRODUCTION

Eucharistic Revival! Have you heard of it? The United States Conference of Catholic Bishops has initiated this national revival as a way of helping Catholics to rediscover the greatest Sacrament of all the sacraments: the Holy Eucharist.

In recent times, surveys and studies have shown that many Catholics — 69 percent, actually — no longer believe in the Real Presence of Jesus Christ in Holy Communion. While there are undoubtedly many reasons for this tragedy in the spiritual lives of Catholics, the Holy Spirit greatly desires to reinvigorate dioceses, parishes, families, religious communities, and all ecclesial groups with a renewed appreciation and love for Our Lord truly present in the Blessed Sacrament.

This book is intended to be an aid to this revival. The specific time-frame set aside by the bishops for a period of the National Eucharistic Revival will come and go, but the Real Presence of Jesus in the Blessed Sacrament will always remain in the tabernacles of Catholic churches around the world. What better way, then, to make sure there always remains an on-going fruit of the Eucharistic Revival than to have a book that offers timeless quotes on the Eucharist — 366 quotes, in fact — from popes, saints, blesseds, venerables, and servants of God? *Eucharistic Gems* is intended to be a book that can be read and re-read for years to come, and keep the Eucharistic Revival ever in our hearts.

Eucharistic Gems is the fourth book in a series published by Marian Press: *Marian Gems, Rosary Gems,* and *St. Joseph Gems.* Family, friends, and people I have met as I travel and speak around the United States have told me that these simple little books have blessed their lives and given them an easy way to be inspired on a daily basis by reading and meditating on the quotes that are presented for each day. These books are truly a delight to put together and I am already gathering quotes for future books: *Sacred Heart Gems* and *Immaculate Heart Gems.*

Composing such a book is not an easy task, though. It requires a lot of work to gather all the quotes and try to arrange them based on the feast days of saints and solemn celebrations in the Church's liturgical calendar. It can be hard to choose what quote to use on a particular day when all the saints love the Eucharist so much and the gems from saints are seemingly without end. When it comes down to it, I try to present the quotes that I consider to be the most extraordinary. For this reason, many of the gems presented come from the same saint or pope, for example, St. Faustina, St. Peter Julian Eymard, Venerable Fulton Sheen, St. John Paul II, etc. When you find a treasure trove of great quotes on the Eucharist, use them!

I pray this book blesses your life. The Holy Eucharist is our greatest treasure and the source of our hope and strength in the spiritual life. The times we live in are filled with fear, anxiety, and worry. As an antidote, take the time to meditate on these daily quotes, pondering the message given throughout your day. Jesus loves you, and he is always waiting for a visit from you in the Blessed Sacrament. Every Catholic Church has a tabernacle; visit him!

One last thing: I would be remiss if I did not acknowledge David Bugajski and the tremendous help he offered in putting this book together. He did a lot of work gathering quotes and also wrote many of the invocations found after each daily quote. I am very grateful to him.

Praised be Jesus Christ in the Most Holy Sacrament of the Altar!

Fr. Donald Calloway, MIC
Vicar Provincial – Marian Fathers of the Immaculate Conception
Blessed Virgin Mary, Mother of Mercy Province

JANUARY

January 1

While the Magi acknowledged and worshipped the baby
that Mary cradled in her arms as the one awaited by
the nations and foretold by prophets, today we can also
worship him in the Eucharist and acknowledge him as our
Creator, our only Lord and Savior.

— POPE BENEDICT XVI

Holy Mary, Mother of God, pray for us!

January 2

It is a sacrament of love, because it was pure love that induced Jesus Christ to give us this gift and pledge of love: for he wished that, should a doubt of his having loved us ever enter into our minds, we should have in this sacrament a pledge of his love.

— St. Alphonsus Liguori

Eucharistic Heart of Jesus, source of justice and love, have mercy on us!

January 3

We beseech you to foster devotion to the Eucharist, which should be the focal point and goal of all other forms of devotion.

— Pope St. Paul VI

Blessed be the name of Jesus!

January 4

Do you suffer from pride? Receive the Eucharist, that is, Christ humbling himself down to the flesh, indeed down to bread, and this humble bread will make you humble. Are you afflicted with the temptation of lust? Receive the wine that generates virgins. Are you afflicted with anger and impatience? Receive Christ crucified, the most patient, and he will give you a share in his patience.

— St. Stanislaus Papczyński

That we may grow in knowledge of this
Sacrament of sacraments, we beseech you, hear us!

January 5

Live on him that you may live for him.

— St. John Vianney

O Blessed Sacrament, cleanse us of sin!

January 6

Nothing contributes more to the spiritual joy and advantage of pious persons than the contemplation of the exalted dignity of this most august Sacrament.

— THE CATECHISM OF THE COUNCIL OF TRENT

That we may make suitable preparation before approaching the altar, we beseech you, hear us!

January 7

Trusting in the mercy of God, though you feel tepid, approach: let him who thinks himself unworthy, reflect, that the more infirm he feels himself, the more he requires a physician.

— ST. BONAVENTURE

By your public ministry Jesus, save your people!

January 8

In the blessed Eucharist is contained the whole spiritual good of the Church.

— CATECHISM OF THE CATHOLIC CHURCH

Sacred Heart of Jesus, protect our families!

January 9

He is not diminished by being given to many, but gives himself whole and entire to each.

— ST. AUGUSTINE OF HIPPO

Blood of Christ, strength of confessors, save us!

January 10

When the chalice we mix and the bread we bake receive the word of God, the Eucharistic elements become the Body and Blood of Christ, by which our bodies live and grow.

— St. Irenaeus

By your Baptism and holy fasting, Lord, save your people!

January 11

Draw strength from receiving this bread as spiritual food and your soul will rejoice.

— St. Cyril of Jerusalem

Blood of Christ, of the New and Eternal Testament, save us!

January 12

Holy Communion is the war that God wages in us against our concupiscence and against the devil, whom our evil passions constantly invite and who, through his connivance with our unruly appetites, holds some part of us in thrall.

— ST. PETER JULIAN EYMARD

Heart of Jesus, well-spring of all virtue, have mercy on us!

January 13

When Our Lord himself declares, as our faith teaches us, that his flesh is food indeed, what room can remain for doubt concerning the Real Presence of his Body and Blood?

— ST. HILARY

Heart of Jesus, I place my trust in you!

January 14

I began to amend my life by frequenting Holy Communion after having tried every other way and failed. When I went rarely to Holy Communion, I had no end of bad habits and imperfections that appeared to me insurmountable. I uprooted these by multiplying my Communions.

— St. Claude de la Colombière

Jesus, model of goodness, have mercy on us!

January 15

By saying that he consecrates himself he means that he offers himself to God as a spotless and sweet-smelling sacrifice. According to the law, anything offered upon the altar was consecrated and considered holy. So Christ gave his own body for the life of all, and makes it the channel through which life flows once more into us.

— St. Cyril of Alexandria

Blood of Christ, relief of the burdened, save us!

January 16

Oh! how wonderful is thy love, O Lord Jesus, who has wished to incorporate us in such a manner with thy body, that we should have one heart and one soul inseparably united with thee.

— St. Lawrence Justinian

Heart of Jesus, one with us in Holy Communion, have mercy on us!

January 17

On the Cross, he would die by the separation of his Blood from his Body. Hence he did not consecrate the bread and wine together, but separately, to show forth the manner of his death by the separation of Body and Blood.

— Venerable Fulton J. Sheen

Lamb of God, you take away the sins of the world, have mercy on us!

January 18

For in Christ's blood we are made strong, even though weakness persists in our sensuality.

— St. Catherine of Siena

Blessed be his most Precious Blood!

January 19

How pleasing to Our Lord in the Blessed Sacrament is the short quarter of an hour that we steal from our occupations, from something of no use, to come and pray to him, to visit him, to console him.

— St. John Vianney

Heart of Jesus, aflame with love for us, have mercy on us!

January 20

I am going to Confession so that I can receive
Holy Communion and then die.

— ST. FRANCISCO MARTO

Lord, have mercy on us, Christ, have mercy on us!

January 21

Live in such a manner as to be able to receive
[Holy Communion] every day.

— ST. AUGUSTINE OF HIPPO

You have redeemed us, O Lord, in your Blood!

January 22

I want to tell you that eternal life must begin already here on earth through Holy Communion. Each Holy Communion makes you more capable of communing with God throughout eternity.

— JESUS TO ST. FAUSTINA KOWALSKA

Jesus, author of life, have mercy on us!

January 23

This most high and adorable Sacrament is the health of body and soul, the remedy for every spiritual disease. By it my vices are cured, my passions bridled, my temptations overcome or diminished; grace is poured out more lavishly in my soul, budding virtue made to bloom, faith made firm, hope strengthened and love set afire and spread abroad.

— THOMAS À KEMPIS

Sweet heart of my Jesus, grant that I may ever love thee more!

January 24

Of truth there is no more loving or tender aspect in which to gaze upon the Savior than this act, in which he, so to say, annihilates himself, and gives himself to us as food, in order to fill our souls, and to unite himself more closely to the heart and the flesh of his faithful ones.

— ST. FRANCIS DE SALES

Jesus, eternal wisdom, have mercy on us!

January 25

The cup of blessing which we bless, is it not a participation in the Blood of Christ? The bread which we break, is it not a participation in the Body of Christ? Because there is one bread, we who are many are one body, for we all partake of the one bread.

— 1 CORINTHIANS 10:16-17

Blood of Christ, pledge of eternal life, save us!

January 26

The Eucharist is my highway to heaven.

— BLESSED CARLO ACUTIS

Lover of our souls in Holy Communion, save us!

January 27

It is not man who makes what is put before him the Body and Blood of Christ, but Christ himself who was crucified for us. The priest standing there in the place of Christ says these words, but their power and grace are from God. "This is my Body," he says, and these words transform what lies before him.

— ST. JOHN CHRYSOSTOM

Blood of Christ, poured out on the cross, save us!

January 28

Devoutly I adore you, hidden Deity, under these appearances concealed. To you my heart surrenders self for, seeing you, all else must yield. Sight and touch and taste here fail; hearing only can be believed. I trust what God's own Son has said.

— St. Thomas Aquinas

Hidden God, have mercy on us!

January 29

Eternal Father, I offer you the Body and Blood, Soul and Divinity of your dearly beloved Son, our Lord Jesus Christ, in atonement for our sins and those of the whole world.

— St. Faustina Kowalska

Blood of Christ, stream of mercy, save us!

January 30

When you hear that I cannot celebrate Mass any more,
count me as dead.

— ST. FRANCIS XAVIER BIANCHI

*Jesus, dwelling in all the tabernacles of the world,
have mercy on us!*

January 31

The flesh born of Mary, coming from the Holy Spirit, is
bread descended from heaven.

— ST. HILARY OF POITIERS

Blood of Christ, victor over demons, save us!

FEBRUARY

Since we have in Holy Communion the grace, the model, and the practice of all the virtues, all of them finding their exercise in this divine action, we shall profit more by Communion than by all other means of sanctification. But to that end, Holy Communion must become the thought that dominates mind and heart.

— St. Peter Julian Eymard

On the day of judgment, Lord, save your people!

February 2

She [Mary] knew her office and her mission:
she accomplished these most faithfully, even to the very
end, by cooperating with the Son as Coredemptrix.
She prepared the Host for sacrifice.

— BLESSED JAMES ALBERIONE

Lord, be merciful. Lord, save your people!

February 3

Nowhere does Jesus hear our prayers more readily than in
the Blessed Sacrament.

— BLESSED HENRY SUSO

More than all men and angels, I love thee, my God!

February 4

Jesus Christ found a way by which he could ascend into heaven and yet remain on the earth. He instituted the adorable Sacrament of the Eucharist so that he might stay with us, and be the food of our soul; that he might console us and be our companion.

— St. John Vianney

Guide and protect your holy Church, Lord!

February 5

Men may hunger for God, but God thirsts for men.

— Venerable Fulton J. Sheen

By your grief and sorrow Jesus, save your people!

February 6

Our mountain hares turn white in winter, because they live in, and feed upon, the snow, and by reason of adoring and feeding upon beauty, goodness, and purity itself in this most divine Sacrament you too will become lovely, holy, pure.

— St. Francis de Sales

Bread of purity, have mercy on us!

February 7

I want adoration to take place for the intention of imploring mercy for the world.

— Jesus to St. Faustina Kowalska

Lamb of God, who takes away the sins of the world, have mercy on us!

February 8

History bears witness that the virtues of the Christian life have flourished best wherever and whenever the frequent reception of the Eucharist has most prevailed. And on the other hand it is no less certain that in days when men have ceased to care for this heavenly bread, and have lost their appetite for it, the practice of Christian religion has gradually lost its force and vigor.

— POPE LEO XIII

Affluence of divine bounty, have mercy on us!

February 9

The Body of Christ drives spiritual illness away and pours in new strength. It is medicinal and nourishing!

— ST. STANISLAUS PAPCZYŃSKI

Body of Christ, strength of the soul, save us!

February 10

Every day at Communion time, I communicate two of my feelings to Jesus. One is gratefulness, because he has helped me to persevere until today. The other is a request: teach me to pray.

— ST. TERESA OF CALCUTTA

From the pride of life, O Lord, deliver us!

February 11

As often as the sacrifice of the Cross in which Christ our Passover was sacrificed is celebrated on the altar, the work of our redemption is carried on, and, in the sacrament of the Eucharistic bread, the unity of all believers who form one body in Christ is both expressed and brought about.

— VATICAN COUNCIL II (*LUMEN GENTIUM*)

Blood of Christ, poured out on the Cross, save us!

February 12

And they held steadfastly to the apostles' teaching and fellowship, to the breaking of the bread and to the prayers.

— ACTS OF THE APOSTLES 2:42

The glorious company of apostles praise you!

February 13

No one can describe the adoration of St. Joseph's noble soul. He saw nothing, yet he believed; his faith had to pierce the virginal veil of Mary. So likewise with you! Under the veil of the Sacred Species your faith must see our Lord. Ask St. Joseph for his lively, constant faith.

— ST. PETER JULIAN EYMARD

By your joy and glory, Jesus, save your people!

February 14

Oh, how painful it is to me that souls so seldom unite themselves to me in Holy Communion. I wait for souls, and they are indifferent toward me. I love them tenderly and sincerely, and they distrust me. I want to lavish my graces on them, and they do not want to accept them. They treat me as a dead object, whereas my heart is full of love and mercy. In order that you may know at least some of my pain, imagine the most tender of mothers who has great love for her children, while those children spurn her love. Consider her pain. No one is in a position to console her. This is but a feeble image and likeness of my love.

— Jesus to St. Faustina Kowalska

Jesus, seeker of souls, have mercy on us!

February 15

In Holy Communion, we receive the same Jesus Christ that
Mary bore for nine months in her womb.

— St. Claude de la Colombière

*Heart of Jesus, from whose fullness we have all received,
have mercy on us!*

February 16

When we come from our Communions, if anyone said to us:
"What are you taking home with you?" we should be able to
reply: "I am carrying away Heaven!"

— St. John Vianney

Jesus, brightness of everlasting light, have mercy on us!

February 17

The Eucharist is the efficacious sign and sublime cause of that communion in the divine life and that unity of the People of God by which the Church is kept in being. It is the culmination both of God"s action sanctifying the world in Christ and of the worship men offer to Christ and through him to the Father in the Holy Spirit.

— CATECHISM OF THE CATHOLIC CHURCH

Holy Trinity, one God, have mercy on us!

February 18

All love craves unity. As the highest peak of love in the human order is the unity of husband and wife in the flesh, so the highest unity in the Divine order is the unity of the soul and Christ in Communion.

— VENERABLE FULTON J. SHEEN

From the spirit of infidelity, Jesus, save your people!

February 19

Before uniting myself to Jesus in the morning through the Eucharist, my heart feels drawn by a power from above. I have such a hunger and thirst for him before receiving him that I am almost breathless.

— ST. PADRE PIO

I repent of having offended you, never permit me to separate myself from you again!

February 20

Our kind Master sees that, unless the fault be our own, this heavenly Bread renders all things easy to us and that we are now capable of fulfilling our promise to the Father of allowing his will to be done in us.

— ST. TERESA OF ÁVILA

Eucharistic Heart of Jesus, loving our hearts, I adore thee!

February 21

If the Eucharist is the source and summit of the Church's life, it is likewise the source and summit of priestly ministry.

— POPE ST. JOHN PAUL II

I love thee, my God!

February 22

If you would give me my Lord three times only,
I should be cured.

— ST. CATHERINE OF GENOA

Eucharistic Heart of Jesus, source of new graces, I adore thee!

February 23

Your watchful care after Communion is no less important than your devout preparation before it. When we keep good watch over ourselves after Communion, it is the best preparation we can make for receiving greater grace. Beware of much talking; stay by yourself in some place apart and there rejoice in the company of your God; there you have him within you, and the whole world cannot take him from you.

— THOMAS À KEMPIS

From the desire of being honored, deliver me, Jesus!

February 24

If you wish to assist at Mass profitably and to secure its many precious fruits, unite yourself as intimately as possible with the Blessed Virgin.

— BLESSED WILLIAM JOSEPH CHAMINADE

Eucharistic Heart of Jesus, sweet refuge of the hidden life, I adore thee!

February 25

The Eucharist is the sacrament of love; it signifies love;
it produces love.

— St. Thomas Aquinas

Jesus, model of obedience, have mercy on us!

February 26

Take great care to go to Holy Mass, even on weekdays;
and for such a cause be willing to put up with some
inconvenience. Thereby you will obtain every kind of
blessing from the Lord.

— St. John Bosco

Precious Blood of Jesus Christ, Scourge of Demons, set us free!

February 27

When we go to Communion, we experience an extraordinary feeling of comfort which seems to envelop us entirely. What is this but Our Lord communicating himself to every part of our being, and making us thrill with joy? We are obliged to exclaim like St. John: "It is the Lord!"

— ST. JOHN VIANNEY

By your sacred mysteries, Lord, save your people!

February 28

Oh, what awesome mysteries take place during Mass! A great mystery is accomplished in the Holy Mass. With what great devotion should we listen to and take part in this death of Jesus. One day we will know what God is doing for us in each Mass, and what sort of gift he is preparing in it for us. Only his divine love could permit that such a gift be provided for us. O Jesus, my Jesus, with what great pain is my soul pierced when I see this fountain of life gushing forth with such sweetness and power for each soul, while at the same time I see souls withering away and drying up through their own fault. O Jesus, grant that the power of mercy embrace these souls.

— ST. FAUSTINA KOWALSKA

Jesus, all-powerful, have mercy on us!

February 29

By celebrating the Last Supper with his apostles in
the course of the Passover meal, Jesus gave the Jewish
Passover its definitive meaning.

— CATECHISM OF THE CATHOLIC CHURCH

Precious Blood of Christ, the Divine Wisdom, save us!

MARCH

March 1

My great delight is to unite myself with souls. Know, my daughter, that when I come to a human heart in Holy Communion, my hands are full of all kinds of graces which I want to give to the soul. But souls do not even pay any attention to me; they leave me to myself and busy themselves with other things. Oh, how sad I am that souls do not recognize love! They treat me as a dead object.

— JESUS TO ST. FAUSTINA KOWALSKA

Heart of Jesus, overwhelmed with insults, have mercy on us!

March 2

We love only that which gives happiness. Seek no further, then. The Savior has placed this divine happiness neither in the different virtues nor in his other mysteries, but solely within himself. To taste his joy to the full, we must receive him as our food.

— St Peter Julian Eymard

Sweet Heart of Jesus, be my love!

March 3

He does not come down from heaven every day to lie in a golden ciborium: He comes to find another heaven which is infinitely dearer to him – the heaven of our souls, created in his image, the living temples of the adorable Trinity!

— St. Thérèse of Lisieux

Lamb without blemish, have mercy on us!

March 4

If I cannot yet become like the Cherubim and Seraphim, I will at least try to be earnest at my devotions and make ready my heart, so that by humbly receiving this life-giving Sacrament I may catch a spark, be it ever so little, of the divine fire.

— THOMAS À KEMPIS

From the desire of being esteemed, deliver me, Jesus!

March 5

I hope in God's goodness, which has never abandoned me on former occasions, will still continue to assist me, and that he and I, we together, will be able to trample under foot all the difficulties which rise up against us. It is a fearsome thing to be in the midst of fallen people, alone, without Mass, without the Sacrifice, without confession, without the Sacraments. Nevertheless, God's holy will and his sweet command on us are well worth that.

— ST. ISAAC JOGUES

Most pure feast, have mercy on us!

March 6

My heart is not like that of others, for it only rejoices in its Lord; and therefore give him to me [in Holy Communion].

— St. Catherine of Genoa

That all priests may have a profound love of the Holy Eucharist, we beseech you, hear us!

March 7

When the life-giving Word of God dwelt in human flesh, he changed it into that good thing which is distinctively his, namely, life; and by being wholly united to the flesh in a way beyond our comprehension, he gave it the life-giving power which he has by his very nature. Therefore, the Body of Christ gives life to those who receive it.

— St. Cyril of Alexandria

Blood of Christ, shed profusely in the scourging, save us!

March 8

Christ our Lord instituted the paschal sacrifice and meal at the Last Supper. In this the sacrifice of the Cross is continually made present in the Church whenever the priest, who represents Christ our Lord, does what Christ himself did and commanded his disciples to do in memory of himself.

— CONSTITUTION ON THE SACRED LITURGY

Worthy is the Lord to receive glory and honor and power: come let us adore!

March 9

By making the bread into his Body and the wine into his Blood, he anticipates his death, he accepts it in his heart, and he transforms it into an action of love. What on the outside is simply brutal violence — the Crucifixion — from within becomes an act of total self-giving love.

— POPE BENEDICT XVI

From anger, hatred, and all ill-will, Lord, save your people!

March 10

For the soul, like the body, needs frequent nourishment; and the Holy Eucharist provides that food which is best adapted to the support of its life.

— POPE LEO XIII

Most august and holy mystery, have mercy on us!

March 11

When we want to obtain anything of the good God, let us, after Holy Communion, offer him his well-beloved Son, with all the merits of his Death and Passion; he will be able to refuse us nothing.

— ST. JOHN VIANNEY

By your death and burial, Jesus, save your people!

March 12

We cannot be fed by that living flesh and hold to the affections of death; and just as our first parents could not die in paradise, because of the tree of life that God had placed therein, so this Sacrament of Life makes spiritual death impossible.

— St. Francis de Sales

Most holy oblation, have mercy on us!

March 13

With what grateful and unspeakable joy and reverence I adore the daily renewed virtue of that word by which we possess him in our blessed Mass and Communion.

— St. Elizabeth Ann Seton

Hidden manna, have mercy on us!

March 14

All the good that is in me is due to Holy Communion.
I owe everything to it. I feel that this holy fire has
transformed me completely. Oh, how happy I am to be a
dwelling place for you, O Lord! My heart is a temple in
which you dwell continually.

— St. Faustina Kowalska

Heart of Jesus, holy temple of God, have mercy on us!

March 15

Only Divine Wisdom could have conceived such a memorial!

— Venerable Fulton J. Sheen

By your rising to new life, Jesus, save your people!

March 16

By the Eucharistic celebration we already unite
ourselves with the heavenly liturgy and anticipate
eternal life, when God will be all in all.

— CATECHISM OF THE CATHOLIC CHURCH

God our Father in heaven, have mercy on us!

March 17

My daily Mass and Communion are my only hope
and resource.

— ST. CLAUDE DE LA COLOMBIÈRE

Blessed be his most Sacred Heart!

March 18

After the spiritual sacrifice, the unbloody act of worship, has been completed, we bend over this propitiatory offering and beg God to grant peace to all the Churches, to give harmony to the whole world, to bless our rulers, our soldiers and our companions, to aid the sick and afflicted, and in general to assist all those who stand in need; we all pray for all these intentions and we offer this victim for them.

— St. Cyril of Jerusalem

Jesus, lover of us all, have mercy on us!

March 19

O God, who has conferred upon us a royal priesthood, we pray to you to give us grace to minister at your holy altars with hearts as clean and lives as blameless as that blessed Joseph who was found to hold in his arms and, with all reverence, carry your only-begotten Son, born of the Virgin Mary. Enable us this day to receive worthily the sacred Body and Blood of your Son, and equip us to win an everlasting reward in the world to come. Amen.

— POPE ST. JOHN PAUL II

St. Joseph, keeper of the Bread, pray for us!

March 20

I shall be made one with him who said unless you eat my flesh and drink my blood you can have no part with me.

— ST. ELIZABETH ANN SETON

My Lord and my God!

March 21

St. Joseph most diligently reared him whom the faithful were to receive as the bread that came down from heaven whereby they might obtain eternal life.

— BLESSED POPE PIUS IX

*Jesus, eternal high priest of the Eucharistic sacrifice,
have mercy on us!*

March 22

When we receive Holy Communion, let us consider that Jesus comes to us as a little baby, and then let us pray that St. Joseph helps us welcome him, as when he held him in his arms.

— ST. JOSEPH MARELLO

Jesus, worthy of our love, have mercy on us!

March 23

If we truly understand the Eucharist; if we make the Eucharist the central focus of our lives; if we feed our lives with the Eucharist, we will not find it difficult to discover Christ, to love him, and to serve him in the poor.

— St. Teresa of Calcutta

Bread of the poor, save us!

March 24

By his incarnation, the Lord has given himself to all men in general; but, in this sacrament, he has given himself to each of us in particular, to make us understand the special love which he entertains for each of us.

— St. Alphonsus Liguori

Sacrament of love, have mercy on us!

March 25

At the Annunciation, Mary conceived the Son of God in the physical reality of his body and blood, thus anticipating within herself what to some degree happens sacramentally in every believer who receives, under the signs of bread and wine, the Lord's Body and Blood.

— POPE ST. JOHN PAUL II

Heart of Jesus, formed by the Holy Spirit in the womb of the Virgin Mother, have mercy on us!

March 26

There is nothing Mary has that is for herself alone — not even her Son. Before he is born, her son belongs to others. No sooner does she have the Divine Host within herself than she rises from the Communion rail of Nazareth to visit the aged [Elizabeth] and to make her young.

— VENERABLE FULTON J. SHEEN

Grant that I may love you always; and then do with me what you will!

March 27

O God, to go and kiss the places you made holy during
your life on earth — the stones of Gethsemane and
Calvary, the ground along the Way of Sorrows, the waves
of the sea of Galilee — but to prefer it to your tabernacle
would be to desert Jesus living besides me, to leave him
alone, going away alone to venerate the dead stones in
places where he is no longer.

— St. Charles de Foucauld

*Christ is the true Lamb that takes away the sins of the world:
come, let us adore!*

March 28

His Majesty has given this food and manna for the children of men once for all, and we can obtain it whenever we please. We shall never die of famine except by our own fault, for the soul that receives the Blessed Sacrament will find in it whatever solace and help it requires.

— St. Teresa of Ávila

Sweetest banquet, at which angels minister, have mercy on us!

March 29

He gave himself to me in Holy Communion far oftener that I should have dared to hope.

— St. Thérèse of Lisieux

Holy, Holy, Holy!

March 30

When we receive Holy Communion,
we receive our joy and happiness.

— ST. JOHN VIANNEY

Jesus, Prince of peace, have mercy on us!

March 31

Although St. Joseph never adored our Lord under
the Eucharistic species and never had the happiness of
communicating [receiving Holy Communion], he did
possess and adore Jesus in human form.

— ST. PETER JULIAN EYMARD

*Eucharistic Heart of Jesus, beating with love for us,
we adore you!*

APRIL

April 1

If his sublime glory could be seen, how could such a
sinful wretch as I am dare to draw near to him after
my many offenses? Beneath the accidents of bread, he
is accessible. If the King disguises himself, there does
not seem to be the same need for ceremonies and court
etiquette; indeed he appears to have waived his claim to
them by appearing incognito.

— St. Teresa of Ávila

From the vice of lust, O Lord, deliver us!

April 2

Jesus in the tabernacle is my God and my all!

— St. Ignatius of Loyola

Come then, Lord, and help your people!

April 3

Partaking of the Body of the Lord in the breaking of the Eucharistic bread, we are taken up into communion with him and with one another.

— VATICAN COUNCIL II (*LUMEN GENTIUM*)

You are God: we praise you!

April 4

I fear the day on which I would not receive Holy Communion. My soul draws astonishing strength from Holy Communion. O living Host, light of my soul!

— ST. FAUSTINA KOWALSKA

Holy Trinity, one God, have mercy on us!

April 5

When Mass was over, I was talking with Jesus and giving him thanks. Oh, how sweet the conversation with paradise. Although I would like to try to explain it all, I cannot. There are things that cannot be put into human language without losing their profound heavenly meaning.

— St. Padre Pio

My beloved Jesus, I embrace the tribulations you have destined for me until death!

April 6

The Eucharist is the sacrament of love par excellence. Certainly the other sacraments are proofs of God's love for us; they are gifts of God. But in the Eucharist, we receive the author of every gift, God himself. So it is in Communion especially that we learn the law of love that our Lord came to reveal. There we receive the special grace of love.

— St. Peter Julian Eymard

Heart of Jesus, source of justice and love, have mercy on us!

April 7

In the sacrament of his Body he actually gives us his own flesh, which he has united to his divinity. This is why we are one, because the Father is in Christ, and Christ is in us. He is in us through his flesh and we are in him.

— St. Hilary

Eucharistic heart of Jesus, eager to grant our requests, I adore thee!

April 8

Holy Communion gives me strength to suffer and fight.

— St. Faustina Kowalska

From the snares of the devil, Jesus, save your people!

April 9

To receive the Blessed Sacrament worthily, one must have a great desire for union with Jesus Christ.

— ST. JOHN VIANNEY

Blood of Christ, most worthy of all glory and honor, save us!

April 10

It is frequently called the *Viaticum* by sacred writers, both because it is spiritual food by which we are sustained in our pilgrimage through this life, and also because it paves our way to eternal glory and happiness.

— THE CATECHISM OF THE COUNCIL OF TRENT

That we may be comforted and sanctified with Holy Viaticum at the hour of our death, we beseech you, hear us!

April 11

Do grant, my God, that when my lips approach yours to kiss you, I may taste the gall that was given to you, when my shoulders lean against yours, make me feel your scourging, when my flesh is united with yours, in the Holy Eucharist, make me feel your Passion; when my head comes near yours, make me feel your thorns; when my heart is close to yours, make me feel your spear.

— St. Gemma Galgani

Jesus, pattern of patience, have mercy on us!

April 12

To withdraw from creatures and repose with Jesus in the tabernacle is my delight; there I can hide myself and seek rest. There I find a life which I cannot describe, a joy which I cannot make others comprehend, a peace such as is found only under the hospitable roof of our best friend.

— St. Ignatius of Loyola

Precious Blood of Jesus Christ, the Sacred Wine, set us free!

April 13

The daily adoration or visit to the Blessed Sacrament is the practice which is the fountainhead of all devotional works.

— Pope St. Pius X

Thou who saves us by thy grace, we beseech thee, hear us!

April 14

He wanted men not to be readers about his redemption, but actors in it, offering up their body and blood with his in the re-enactment of Calvary, saying with him, "This is my body and this is my blood," dying to their lower natures to live to grace, saying that they cared not for the appearance or species of their lives such as their family relationships, jobs, duties, physical appearance, or talents, but that their intellects, their wills, their substance — all that they truly were — would be changed into Christ; that the Heavenly Father looking down on them would see them in his Son, see their sacrifices massed in his sacrifice, their mortifications incorporated with his death, so that eventually they might share in his glory.

— VENERABLE FULTON J. SHEEN

By your abandonment, Jesus, save your people!

April 15

The priest should have the same joy as the apostles in seeing our Lord whom he holds in his hands.

— ST. JOHN VIANNEY

By your agony and crucifixion, Jesus, save your people!

April 16

I consider that it is the holy Virgin who gives me the Baby Jesus [Holy Communion]. I receive him. I speak to him and he speaks to me.

— ST. BERNADETTE SOUBIROUS

Jesus, Bread of life, have mercy on us!

April 17

When he was at table with them, he took the bread and blessed and broke it, and gave it to them. And their eyes were opened and they recognized him; and he vanished out of their sight. They said to each other, "did not our hearts burn within us while he talked to us on the road, while he opened to us the Scriptures?" And they rose that same hour and returned to Jerusalem; and they found the eleven gathered together and those who were with them, who said, "The Lord has risen indeed, and has appeared to Simon!" Then they told them what had happened on the road, and how he was known to them in the breaking of the bread.

— LUKE 24: 30-35

By your holy resurrection, Lord, save your people!

April 18

If I had to go miles and miles over burning coals in order to receive Jesus, I would say the way was easy, as if I were walking on a carpet of roses.

— ST. CATHERINE OF GENOA

Jesus, victim, I wish to console thee!

April 19

In her daily preparation for Calvary, Mary experienced a kind of "anticipated Eucharist" — one might say a "spiritual communion" — of desire and of oblation, which would culminate in her union with her Son in his Passion, and then find expression after Easter by her partaking in the Eucharist which the Apostles celebrated as the memorial of that Passion.

— POPE ST. JOHN PAUL II

Eucharistic Heart of Jesus, desiring to be loved, I adore thee!

April 20

This is what I pray for, long for: to be made wholly one with you, to withdraw my heart from all created things, and through Holy Communion learn more to delight in heavenly and eternal things.

— THOMAS À KEMPIS

From the desire of being praised, deliver me, Jesus!

April 21

Thank you for the good gift of this your holy Body and Blood, which I desire to receive, as a cleansing from sin, and for the defense against it. Lord, I acknowledge that I am far from worthy to approach and touch this sacrament; but I trust that mercy which caused you to lay down your life for sinners that they might be justified, and because you gave yourself willingly as a holy sacrifice to the Father.

— ST. ANSELM OF CANTERBURY

Jesus, Son of the Living God, hear our prayer!

April 22

The Eucharist is something more than simply receiving Christ. It supposes that we satisfy his hunger. Christ invites us, "Come to me." Christ hungers for souls.

— St. Teresa of Calcutta

For those who turn to you in their last hour, Lord, have mercy!

April 23

Do not injure Jesus, my child, for the coldness of men, the ingratitude of souls and the solitude of the tabernacle still wound him with bitter disappointment.

— Blessed Concepción Cabrera de Armida

Blood of Christ, price of our salvation, save us!

April 24

In this most admirable Sacrament, which is the chief means whereby men are engrafted on the divine nature, men also find the most efficacious help towards progress in every kind of virtue.

— POPE LEO XIII

Medicine of immortality, save us!

April 25

And as they were eating, he took bread, and blessed, and broke it, and gave it to them, and said, "Take; this is my Body." And he took a chalice, and when he had given thanks he gave it to them, and they all drank of it. And he said to them, "This is my Blood of the new covenant, which is poured out for many. Truly, I say to you, I shall not drink again of the fruit of the vine until that day when I drink it new in the kingdom of God."

— MARK 14: 22-25

Chalice of salvation, save us!

April 26

O my Jesus, I understand the meaning of "host," the meaning of sacrifice. I desire to be before your Majesty a living host; that is, a living sacrifice that daily burns in your honor. When my strength begins to fail, it is Holy Communion that will sustain me and give me strength.

— St. Faustina Kowalska

Strengthen and preserve us in your holy service, Lord, hear our prayer!

April 27

Happier than those who lived during his mortal life, when he was only in one place, we find Jesus Christ today in every corner of the world, in the Blessed Sacrament.

— St. John Vianney

God the Son, Redeemer of the world, have mercy on us!

April 28

Always remember that the more you allow Mary to act in
your Communion, the more Jesus will be glorified.

— ST. LOUIS DE MONTFORT

Divine sacrifice of love, have mercy on us!

April 29

Oh sweet blood, you strip us of selfish sensual love that
weakens those who wear it, and you clothe us in the fire
of divine charity.

— ST. CATHERINE OF SIENA

Blood of Christ, flowing forth in the crowning with thorns,
save us!

April 30

The bread itself and the wine are made over into the
Body and Blood of God.

— St. John Damascene

Memorial of the wonders of God, have mercy on us!

MAY

May 1

Saint Joseph is still charged with guarding the Living Bread!
— VENERABLE FULTON J. SHEEN

St. Joseph, Guardian of the Heavenly Manna, pray for us!

May 2

He has done us a great grace by teaching us that he is present in the Blessed Sacrament. But he will not show himself openly or reveal his glories or bestow his treasures, save on souls which prove that they ardently desire him, for these are his real friends.

— ST. TERESA OF ÁVILA

Supersubstantial bread, have mercy on us!

May 3

Prayer made in union with this divine sacrifice has untold power.

— St. Francis de Sales

Delight of angels, save us!

May 4

Oh! how ardently does Jesus desire to come to our souls in Holy Communion!

— St. Alphonsus Liguori

By the gift of the Holy Eucharist, Jesus, save your people!

May 5

The two sacraments of the Eucharist and Penance are very closely connected. Because the Eucharist makes present the redeeming sacrifice of the Cross, perpetuating it sacramentally, it naturally gives rise to a continuous need for conversion. If a Christian's conscience is burdened by serious sin, then the path of penance through the sacrament of Reconciliation becomes necessary for full participation in the Eucharistic Sacrifice.

— POPE ST. JOHN PAUL II

Chalice of benediction, have mercy on us!

May 6

Nothing is more efficacious than a good Communion, whether in avoiding sin, or in preserving and augmenting the grace that we have had the happiness to receive.

— ST. IGNATIUS OF LOYOLA

True propitiation for the living and the dead, have mercy on us!

May 7

The inexhaustible riches of this Sacrament is expressed in the different names we give it. Each name evokes certain aspects of it. It is called: Eucharist, because it is an action of thanksgiving to God. The Greek word *eucharistein* and *eulogein* recall the Jewish blessings that proclaim – especially during a meal – God's works: creation, redemption and sanctification.

— CATECHISM OF THE CATHOLIC CHURCH

Gift transcending all fullness, have mercy on us!

May 8

The minutes that follow Communion are the most precious we have in our lives. They are the minutes best suited on our part for being with God, and on his part for communicating his love to us.

— ST. MARY MAGDALENE DE 'PAZZI

That we may cherish time spent in silent prayer before you, we beseech you, hear us!

May 9

By this Sacrament our hope of everlasting blessedness,
based on our trust in the divine assistance, is
wonderfully strengthened.

— POPE LEO XIII

*Precious Blood of Jesus Christ, the Power of Christians,
set us free!*

May 10

The body of Christ that the most Blessed Virgin bore,
fostered in her bosom, wrapped in swaddling cloths, and
nurtured with maternal love, that body, I say, and without
doubt not any other, we now receive from the holy altar, and
we drink his blood as a sacrament of our redemption.

— ST. PETER DAMIAN

All you holy disciples of the Lord, pray for us!

May 11

When we cannot come to church, let us turn towards
the tabernacle and make a spiritual Communion. A wall
cannot separate us from God.

— St. John Vianney

*Heart of Jesus, treasure-house of wisdom and knowledge,
have mercy on us!*

May 12

He [Jesus] was Blessed Mary's food, her Son, the honey of
angels, the sweetness of all the saints. Her life was sustained
by him whom she fed. The Son, to whom she gave milk to
drink, gave her life.

— St. Anthony of Padua

God will guard us from all harm: let us give thanks and praise!

May 13

Devotion to the Blessed Sacrament and devotion to the Blessed Virgin are not simply the best way, but in fact are the only way to conserve purity. At the age of twenty, nothing but Communion can keep one's heart pure.

— St. Philip Neri

You Christ, are the King of glory!

May 14

O my child, those Christians who are lost will indeed have no answer to give when the Just Judge sets before them that they have voluntarily died the spiritual death, since it was easy for them to have preserved life and health, by eating his Body that he gave them for that very end.

— St. Francis de Sales

Refreshment of holy souls, have mercy on us!

May 15

You are there, my Lord Jesus, in the Holy Eucharist. You are there but a few feet from me, in the tabernacle. Your body, your soul, your humanity, your divinity, your entire being is there in its double nature! How close you are, God!

— ST. CHARLES DE FOUCAULD

Let us thank the Lord for his love!

May 16

I am the same under each of the species, but not every soul receives me with the same living faith as you do, my daughter, and therefore I cannot act in their souls as I do in yours.

— JESUS TO ST. FAUSTINA KOWALSKA

Jesus, worthy of our wonder, have mercy on us!

May 17

God is really present in the consecrated Host as he is in the glory of heaven.

— St. Paschal Baylon

For those who do not believe in your Eucharistic Presence, have mercy, O Lord!

May 18

Concerning Holy Communion, I hardly dare to say anything, because of the majesty of so great a Lord who is contained therein. Consider that you are approaching God, before whom all majesty becomes insignificant and all wisdom vanishes. Yet because he is of unbounded goodness, he not only kindly waits for you, but — what is more — calls you to himself, so that he may cleanse and sanctify your inner being by the sharing of himself.

— St. Stanislaus Papczyński

Lord, be merciful. Lord, save your people!

May 19

Sometimes I think of those devout folk, Lord, who approach
this Sacrament of yours with utmost devotion and love; and
many a time I blush for myself, feel guilty within me, to
think that when I approach your altar, the table of your Holy
Communion, I do so with my heart so cold and lacking in
fervor. I am ashamed that I remain so dry, so void of love.

— THOMAS À KEMPIS

From the desire of being preferred to others, deliver me, Jesus!

May 20

Who of us is ignorant of the countless outrages done the
Catholic religion and of the unheard-of blasphemies of which
its adorable author is the constant object in many parts of the
world? Christ and his religion are outraged by forgetfulness
of evangelical truths and abandonment of the sacraments.
The Church is outraged by the vast plan of persecution
hatched for many years and in many countries against
bishops and priests. Religion is outraged by the battering
down of crosses and the profanation of churches. Worse than
these outrages, from those who have never been of the true
fold and who have grown up in the abuse of grace and that
almost universal hardness of heart so characteristic of this
generation, are the outrages of hypocritical sinners who go to
Communion unworthily and sacrilegiously.

— BLESSED BASIL MOREAU

Give thanks to the Lord, for he is good,
for his mercy endures forever!

May 21

Through the words of consecration the substance of bread and wine is changed into your Body and Blood. Oh, Omnipotent Lord, consecrate me, speak over me, and change me into thee.

— St. Anthony Mary Claret

I love you, my beloved Jesus. I love you more than myself!

May 22

O sacred banquet, in which Christ is received, the memory of his Passion is renewed, the mind is filled with grace, and a pledge of future glory is given to us.

— St. Thomas Aquinas

I accept in particular the death you have destined for me, with all the pains that may accompany it! I unite it to your death; I offer it to you!

May 23

I believe in my heart and openly profess that the bread and wine that are placed on the altar are, through the mystery of the sacred prayer and the words of the Redeemer, substantially changed into the true and proper and life-giving flesh and blood of Jesus Christ our Lord, and that after the consecration they are the true body of Christ — which was born of the Virgin and which hung on the Cross as an offering for the salvation of the world — and the true blood of Christ — which flowed from his side — and not just as a sign and by reason of the power of the sacrament, but in the very truth and reality of their substance and in what is proper to their nature.

— St. Gregory VII

Jesus, our God, have mercy on us!

May 24

O my Jesus, may I help to make you known to all; may I cause you to be adored, loved, and thanked at every moment in your most holy and divine Sacrament of love.

— BLESSED BASIL MOREAU

Blood of Christ, without which there is no forgiveness, save us!

May 25

The soul that receives the Divine Blood becomes beautiful, for it is clothed in a more precious garment, and it appears so resplendently aglow that, if you could see it, you would be tempted to adore it.

— ST. MARY MAGDALENE DE' PAZZI

*Sacred Host, source and summit of all worship,
have mercy on us!*

May 26

Chastity is not possible without the Eucharist.

— ST. PHILIP NERI

By your return in glory, Jesus, save your people!

May 27

To those who say they admire my courage, I have to tell them that I would not have any if I were not convinced that each time I touch the body of a leper, a body that reeks with foul stench, I touch Christ's body, the same Christ I receive in the Eucharist.

— ST. TERESA OF CALCUTTA

By your holy death, deliver us, O Jesus!

May 28

The leaven of our former malice is thrown out, and a new creature is filled and inebriated with the Lord himself. For the effect of our sharing in the body and blood of Christ is to change us into what we receive. As we have died with him, and have been buried and raised to life in him, so we bear him within us, both in body and in spirit, in everything we do.

— ST. LEO THE GREAT

Heart of Jesus, full of goodness and love, have mercy on us!

May 29

Just as the sun cannot be divided, so neither can my wholeness as God and as man in this white host. It is just as when a mirror is broken, and yet the image one sees reflected in it remains unbroken. So when this host is divided, I am not divided but remain completely in each piece, wholly God, wholly man.

— JESUS TO ST. CATHERINE OF SIENA

Reward all our benefactors with eternal blessings, Lord, hear our prayer!

May 30

I seem to be in danger of death from this malady; if it be the pleasure of God that I die here, I beg that I may be heard in Confession and also receive my Savior; and that I may be buried in consecrated ground.

— St. Joan of Arc

Blood of Christ, help of those in peril, save us!

May 31

Mary also anticipated, in the mystery of the incarnation, the Church's Eucharistic faith. When, at the Visitation, she bore in her womb the Word made flesh, she became in some way a "tabernacle" — the first "tabernacle" in history — in which the Son of God, still invisible to our human gaze, allowed himself to be adored by Elizabeth, radiating his light as it were through the eyes and the voice of Mary.

— Pope St. John Paul II

Heart of Jesus, tabernacle of the Most High, have mercy on us!

JUNE

No one may share the Eucharist with us unless he believes that what we teach is true, unless he is washed in the regenerating waters of baptism for the remission of his sins, and unless he lives in accordance with the principles given us by Christ.

— ST. JUSTIN MARTYR

Precious Blood of Jesus, our defense against evil, set us free!

June 2

Two things constitute my heaven on earth: The holy will of God and the Most Blessed Sacrament!

— BLESSED CRESCENTIA OF KAUFBEUREN

On the Day of Judgment, have mercy on us, Lord!

June 3

To give us life, he made himself the Bread of Life. In this Sacrament of Love, Jesus continually offers long life and faithful personal friendship. To make this love more real, he gives his body to be our Bread of Life.

— St. Teresa of Calcutta

You are the Lord: we acclaim you!

June 4

O Heart of Jesus, Heart outraged by incredulity, by forgetfulness, and by the contradictions of mankind, have pity still on your heritage, and do not abandon it to the fury of your enemies. We know well that not all these enemies are those who do not know you or who deny your presence among us; some of them even partake of your sacred banquet with cold and indifferent souls or even with souls infected by hideous leprosy of sin, thus wounding your Heart most dolorously even in the house of those who love you.

— Blessed Basil Moreau

God our Father in Heaven, have mercy on us!

June 5

Each Holy Communion brought about is truly an immeasurable gain. Through the individual soul, it nourishes the entire Mystical Body of Christ.

— SERVANT OF GOD FRANK DUFF

God the Holy Spirit, have mercy on us!

June 6

The Savior instituted the most holy Sacrament of the Eucharist, really containing his Body and his Blood, in order that they who eat it might live forever. And therefore whosoever receives it frequently and devoutly, so strengthens the health and life of his soul, that it is hardly possible for him to be poisoned by any evil desires.

— ST. FRANCIS DE SALES

Sacrament of piety, have mercy on us!

June 7

No one can fail to see that the divine Eucharist bestows an incomparable dignity upon the Christian people. For it is not just while the Sacrifice is being offered and the Sacrament is being confected, but also after the Sacrifice has been offered and the Sacrament confected — while the Eucharist is reserved in churches or oratories — that Christ is truly Emmanuel, which means "God with us." For he is in the midst of us day and night; he dwells in us with the fullness of grace and of truth.

— POPE ST. PAUL VI

Jesus, our way and our life, have mercy on us!

June 8

When you think of going to Mass on working days, it is an impulse of the grace that God wills to grant you. Follow it.

— ST. JOHN VIANNEY

Heart of Jesus, atonement for our sins, have mercy on us!

June 9

Wherever I may be I will often think of Jesus in the Blessed Sacrament. I will fix my thoughts on the holy tabernacle — even when I happen to wake up at night — adoring him from where I am, calling to Jesus in the Blessed Sacrament, offering up to him the action in which I am engaged. I will install one telegraph cable from my study to the church, another from my bedroom, and a third from our refectory; and as often as I can, I will send messages of love to Jesus in the Blessed Sacrament.

— VENERABLE ANDREW BELTRAMI

Memorial of divine love, have mercy on us!

June 10

Before the Blessed Sacrament I feel an inexplicably lively faith. I almost become sensible of the wounds of Jesus and long to kiss them. When the hour for leaving the Divine Presence comes, I must make every effort to resist the inclination of remaining there longer.

— St. Anthony Mary Claret

Let us thank the Lord for his love!

June 11

The soul in its natural life, must live forever; it has received that immortality from God. But the life of grace received in Baptism, and regained and renewed in the sacrament of Penance, that life of sanctity, more noble by far than the natural life, cannot be maintained without sustenance; and its principle nutriment is the Eucharistic Jesus.

— St. Peter Julian Eymard

Holy Sacrament, life of the soul, save us!

June 12

Take pleasure in remaining in his company: do not lose this most precious time, for this hour is of the utmost value to the soul, and the good Jesus desires you to spend it with him.

— St. Teresa of Ávila

From lust of the eyes, O Lord, deliver us!

June 13

Give him to me; I long for him [in Holy Communion], and I cannot live without him.

— St. Gemma Galgani

Eucharistic Heart of Jesus, teaching the secrets of divine union, I adore thee!

June 14

O rose of my heart, which I am moved to kiss and caress! O Eucharist of my life, light of my existence, my white Bread descending from heaven through Mary! Come and drown me in the source of your infinite love. How much I owe you!

— BLESSED CONCEPCIÓN CABRERA DE ARMIDA

May the Sacred Heart of Jesus be loved in every place!

June 15

After Holy Communion, when I had welcomed Jesus into my heart, I said to him, "My Love, reign in the most secret recesses of my heart, there where my most secret thoughts are conceived, where you alone have free access, in this deepest sanctuary where human thought cannot penetrate. May you alone dwell there, and may everything I do exteriorly take its origin in you. I ardently desire, and I am striving with all the strength of my soul, to make you, Lord, feel at home in this sanctuary."

— ST. FAUSTINA KOWALSKA

Heart of Jesus, desire of the eternal hills, have mercy on us!

June 16

To induce us to receive him frequently in Holy Communion, he promises eternal life — that is, the kingdom of Heaven — to those who eat his flesh.

— ST. ALPHONSUS LIGUORI

Blood of Christ, freeing souls from Purgatory, save us!

June 17

If only you would enkindle me with the fire of your presence, consume me with those flames, change me into yourself! So, by the grace of that inward union, that melting away beneath the heat of burning love, you and I would become a single spirit.

— THOMAS À KEMPIS

God is our portion and our cup: come, let us adore!

June 18

The bread and the wine are not a type of the Body and Blood of Christ — perish the thought! — but the deified Body itself of the Lord, since the Lord himself has said: "This is my Body." He did not say a type of his Body, but his Body; not a type of his Blood, but his Blood.

— ST. JOHN DAMASCENE

Rejoice, O hearts that seek the Lord!

June 19

This [the Sacrifice of the Mass] is the memorial most sweet and salvific in which we gratefully recall the memory of our redemption, the memorial in which we attain the corporeal presence of the Savior himself.

— POPE URBAN IV

In time and eternity, I love thee, my God!

June 20

I will only say that when I am with Jesus in the Blessed Sacrament, the beating of my heart is so strong that it sometimes seems my heart is bursting out of my chest. At the altar at times I feel such a burning throughout my whole being that I cannot describe it. It seems to me that my face is completely on fire.

— ST. PADRE PIO

Let us adore forever — the Most Blessed Sacrament!

June 21

He has done all that he could to aid them, as his own children, while they lived on earth, dwelling with them and strengthening them. If they are overcome he will not be to blame, for he never ceased to encourage them until the end of the fray. Lost souls will have no excuse to make for themselves, nor will they be able to accuse Christ's Father of depriving them of this Bread in their direst need.

— St. Teresa of Ávila

Jesus, victim! I wish to annihilate myself before thee!

June 22

It is pleasant to spend time with him, to lie close to his breast like the Beloved Disciple and to feel the intimate love present in his heart. If in our time Christians must be distinguished above all by the "art of prayer," how can we not feel a renewed need to spend time in spiritual converse, in silent adoration, in heartfelt love before Christ in the Most Blessed Sacrament?

— POPE ST. JOHN PAUL II

Heart of Jesus, Son of the eternal Father, have mercy on us!

June 23

Motivated by his own love and by his desire to teach us to love, Jesus came on earth and has stayed with us in the Eucharist.

— ST. JOSEMARIA ESCRIVÁ

Innocent Lamb of God, have mercy on us!

June 24

If we were more fervent Christians, we would experience, in the presence of Jesus Christ on our altars, what John the Baptist experienced in the presence of Jesus Christ resting in Mary's womb.

— BLESSED WILLIAM JOSEPH CHAMINADE

Most Sacred Heart of Jesus, may the whole world burn with love for you!

June 25

My delights are to be with the children of men. To satisfy my love I have obliged myself to remain therein even to the end of the world, and I wish it [the Holy Eucharist] to be frequently received. Should anyone deter a soul in the state of grace from Communion, he would impede the delight of my heart. I have done my utmost to manifest the tenderness of my heart in the Blessed Eucharist.

— JESUS TO ST. GERTRUDE

Sacred Heart of Jesus, I have confidence in thee!

June 26

When we leave the holy banquet of Communion, we are as happy as the wise men would have been if they could have carried away the Infant Jesus.

— ST. JOHN VIANNEY

Jesus, King of glory, have mercy on us!

June 27

For Christ is not altered and his holy Body is not changed; instead the power and force and life-giving grace of the blessing remain in it forever.

— ST. CYRIL OF ALEXANDRIA

Heart of Jesus, fountain of life and holiness, have mercy on us!

June 28

If our flesh is not saved, then the Lord has not redeemed us with his blood, the Eucharistic chalice does not make us sharers in his blood, and the bread we break does not make us sharers in his body. There can be no blood without veins, flesh and the rest of the human substance, and this the Word of God actually became: it was with his own blood that he redeemed us.

— St. Irenaeus

Blood of Christ, consolation of the dying, save us!

June 29

You know that you were ransomed from the futile ways
inherited from your fathers, not with perishable things such
as silver or gold, but with the precious blood of Christ, like
that of a lamb without blemish or spot. He was destined
before the foundation of the world but was made manifest at
the end of times for your sake.

— 1 PETER 1:18-20

Saints Peter and Paul, pray for us!

June 30

This Sacrament is not only a sacrament of love, but is love
itself; it is God himself, who for the immense love which he
bears his creatures, calls himself, and is, love itself.

— ST. ALPHONSUS LIGUORI

Eucharistic Heart of Jesus, have mercy on us!

JULY

July 1

July 1

Your main intention in Communion should be to grow, strengthen, and abound in the love of God; for love's sake receive that which love alone gives you.

— ST. FRANCIS DE SALES

May we be clothed with Christ!

July 2

Never deliberately miss Holy Communion. Communion is more than life, more than all the good things of the world, more than the whole universe: it is God himself, it is I, Jesus. Could you prefer anything to me? Could you, if you love me at all, however little, voluntarily lose grace I give you in this way? Love me in all the breath and simplicity of your heart.

— JESUS TO ST. CHARLES DE FOUCAULD

Lord, let your love come upon me!

July 3

Our reception of Holy Communion should become more perfect each day, so that the last, which we will receive as Viaticum, will be the most consoling, the most fervent, the one that will prepare us for our everlasting union with God.

— BLESSED JAMES ALBERIONE

*Eucharistic Heart of Jesus, desirous of being sought,
I adore thee!*

July 4

Since our Divine Lord came to die, it was fitting that there be a memorial of his death! Since he was God, as well as man, and since he never spoke of his death without speaking of his Resurrection, should he not himself institute the precise memorial of his own death and leave it to the chance recollection of men? And this is exactly what he did the night of the Last Supper.

— VENERABLE FULTON J. SHEEN

Blessed be God!

July 5

No one will be in Christ unless Christ himself has been in him; Christ will take to himself only the flesh of those who have received his flesh.

— St. Hilary

Jesus, father of the world to come, have mercy on us!

July 6

After this [First Communion], I'll get better and better.

— St. Maria Goretti

All you holy virgins, pray for us!

July 7

He is hidden from our eyes under the humility of his Sacrament, to try our faith.

— ST. JOHN VIANNEY

Jesus, gentle and humble of heart, touch our hearts and make them like your own!

July 8

Most Holy Trinity — Father, Son, and Holy Spirit — I adore thee profoundly. I offer thee the most precious Body, Blood, Soul and Divinity of Jesus Christ, present in all the tabernacles of the world, in reparation for the outrages, sacrileges and indifferences whereby he is offended. And through the infinite merits of his Most Sacred Heart and the Immaculate Heart of Mary, I beg of thee the conversion of poor sinners.

— ANGEL OF PEACE, THE GUARDIAN ANGEL OF PORTUGAL, TO THE THREE CHILDREN AT FÁTIMA

All you Holy Angels and Archangels, pray for us!

July 9

When you are attending Mass and other religious services, be very reverent when you stand up, kneel, and sit. Perform each action with great devotion. Be modest in your gaze, and do not turn your head this way and that to see who is coming or going. Out of reverence for that holy place, do not laugh or look around to see who is nearby. Try not to talk to anyone unless charity or a strict need requires it.

— St. Padre Pio

Blessed be God forever!

July 10

If the Church and the Eucharist are inseparably united, the same ought to be said of Mary and the Eucharist.

— Pope St. John Paul II

Most holy commemoration of the Passion of Christ, have mercy on us!

July 11

Why is it [the Lord's Prayer] spoken before the reception of Christ's Body and Blood? For the following reason: If perchance, in consequence of human frailty, our thought seized on something indecent, if our tongue spoke something unjust, if our eye was turned to something unseemly, if our ear listened complacently to something unnecessary it is blotted out by the Lord's Prayer in the passage: Forgive us our debts, so that we may approach in peace and so that we may not eat or drink what we receive unto judgment.

— St. Augustine of Hippo

Thou who art Infinite Love, I love thee, my God!

July 12

He instituted this adorable Sacrament in order to remain with us to the end.

— Blessed Basil Moreau

Jesus, gentle and humble of heart, have mercy on us!

July 13

I find my consolation in the only companion of mine
who never leaves me, that is, our divine Savior in the
Holy Eucharist.

— ST. DAMIEN OF MOLOKAI

Thou who didst first love me. I love thee, my God!

July 14

Beg him not to fail you but to give you the grace
to receive him worthily. Since you have completely
abandoned yourselves into the hands of God, have no
care for any other bread but this.

— ST. TERESA OF ÁVILA

*Grant that in all temptations which assail me I may always
commend myself to you!*

July 15

There is no difficulty over Christ's being present in the sacrament as in a sign; the great difficulty is in the fact that he is really in the Sacrament, as he is in heaven. And so believing this is especially meritorious.

— St. Bonaventure

Heart of Jesus, house of God and gate of heaven, have mercy on us!

July 16

Experiencing the memorial of Christ's death in the Eucharist also means continually receiving this gift. It means accepting — like John — the one who is given to us anew as our Mother. It also means taking on a commitment to be conformed to Christ, putting ourselves at the school of his Mother and allowing her to accompany us. Mary is present, with the Church and as the Mother of the Church, at each of our celebrations of the Eucharist.

— Pope St. John Paul II

Word made flesh, dwelling in us, have mercy on us!

July 17

Hence it also follows that Christ is so contained, whole and entire, under either species, that as under the species of bread are contained not only the Body, but also the Blood, and Christ entire; so in like manner, under the species of wine are truly contained not only the Blood, but also the Body, and Christ entire.

— THE CATECHISM OF THE COUNCIL OF TRENT

Blood of Christ, falling upon the earth in the agony, save us!

July 18

We celebrate the memory of the Pasch of Christ, and of that night when he wished to share with his brothers the lamb and the unleavened bread, according to the instructions given to their forefathers. After the figurative lamb, the meal being finished, we confess that the Body of the Lord was given with his own hands to the disciples, entirely to all and entirely to each.

— ST. THOMAS AQUINAS

Adoration be to the Most Holy Trinity!

July 19

All who are deeply conscious of the Real Presence make it visible in a thousand different ways in their external behavior, their movements, their posture, and especially by where they look, keeping their sight devoutly on the Sacred Host.

— BLESSED BASIL MOREAU

Blessed be Jesus Christ, true God and true Man!

July 20

To be alone with Jesus in adoration and intimate union with him is the greatest gift of love – the tender love of our Father in Heaven. The fruit of our daily adoration is that our love for Jesus is more intimate, our love for each other is more understanding, our love for the poor is more compassionate, and we have doubled the number of vocations. So let us be all for Jesus through Mary.

— ST. TERESA OF CALCUTTA

All families of the nations worship before the Lord: come, let us adore!

July 21

The Mass is my heaven on Earth.

— ST. LAWRENCE BRINDISI

Precious Blood of Jesus Christ, the Divine Charity, set us free!

July 22

Our very body will receive in Communion a pledge of resurrection, and, even in this life it will be more temperate, more obedient to the soul. It will but take its rest in the tomb, conserving the Eucharistic seed, source of a more splendid glory for it in the day of eternal reward.

— ST. PETER JULIAN EYMARD

*Lamb of God, who takes away the sins of the world,
spare us, O Lord!*

July 23

Every time people approach the sacred table, and especially those who prepare themselves most attentively to receive the Holy Sacrament, they are filled by God with countless gifts, they receive unheard-of and inconceivable graces; they are sanctified, strengthened, and obtain the forgiveness of evil deeds and the promise of eternal life.

— St. Stanislaus Papczyński

Holy Sacrament, greatest of all gifts, save us!

July 24

The Holy Eucharist is no mere symbol of him, or instrument of his power, but is Jesus Christ himself substantially.

— Servant of God Frank Duff

Let us hope in God and praise him still,
our Savior and our God!

July 25

The miracles of the multiplication of the loaves, when the Lord says the blessing, breaks and distributes the loaves through the disciples to feed the multitude, prefigure the superabundance of this unique bread of his Eucharist. The sign of water turned into wine at Cana already announces the Hour of Jesus' glorification. It makes manifest the fulfillment of the wedding feast in the Father's kingdom, where the faithful will drink the new wine that has become the Blood of Christ.

— CATECHISM OF THE CATHOLIC CHURCH

Throughout the world the holy Church acclaims you!

July 26

The human heart craves contact with the beloved. If we can have contact with nature through the food we eat; if lower creation winds up somehow inside of my body, why should not means be provided in order that there might be communion of the soul? This is one of the first effects of Holy Communion: we receive from Christ what we gave to him. We gave to him our human nature — when, in the name of humanity, Mary gave him manhood, like unto us in all things save sin. He divinized that human nature because it was made substantially one with his Divine Person. In Communion, he gives it back to us, purified, regenerated, ennobled, and a promise and a pledge of what our nature is to be on the Last Day in the resurrection of the just.

— Venerable Fulton J. Sheen

Precious Blood of Jesus Christ, the Armor of God, set us free!

July 27

And why does Jesus Christ so vehemently desire that we receive him in Holy Communion? It is because he takes delight in being united with each of us. By Communion, Jesus is really united to our soul and to our body, and we are united to Jesus.

— St. Alphonsus Liguori

Jesus, lover of chastity, have mercy on us!

July 28

To what outrages does our Lord expose himself in the Blessed Sacrament that he may remain in the midst of us! He is there to console us, and therefore we ought to visit him.

— St. John Vianney

Heart of Jesus, broken for our sins, have mercy on us!

July 29

This then is what Christ intended when he instituted this Venerable Sacrament, namely, by awakening charity towards God to promote mutual charity among men. For the latter, as is plain, is by its very nature rooted in the former, and springs from it by a kind of spontaneous growth. Nor is it possible that there should be any lack of charity among men, or rather it must needs be enkindled and flourish, if men would but ponder well the charity which Christ has shown in this Sacrament.

— POPE LEO XIII

Tremendous and life-giving Sacrament, have mercy on us!

July 30

Let us make frequent and devout visits to God in the tabernacle.

— BLESSED JAMES ALBERIONE

With all my mind, I love thee, my God!

July 31

The Eucharist is the flesh of our Savior Jesus Christ which
suffered for our sins and which the Father in his loving
kindness raised again.

— ST. IGNATIUS OF LOYOLA

Be merciful to us sinners, Lord, hear our prayer!

AUGUST

"But I say unto you, none of those men that were invited shall taste my supper" (Lk. 14:26). This supper is Holy Communion: it is a great supper, at which all the faithful are invited to eat the sacred flesh of Jesus Christ in the most Holy Sacrament of the altar.

— St. Alphonsus Liguori

Blood of Christ, Eucharistic drink and refreshment of souls, save us!

August 2

I will go even further and affirm that by Communion we are raised above the angels, if not in nature, at least in honor. In receiving our Lord, do we not become his brethren, other Christs? The angels are only his ministers. When we have received him in Communion, oh, with what veneration they gather round us, what honor they show us! In this respect, Communion enhances our worth even beyond what we would have possessed without Original Sin. Innocent, we would have been forever below the angels; regenerated and having become, through the Eucharist, of the same blood with Jesus Christ, we are given the right to occupy a higher throne in heaven then the celestial spirits. And the more we receive Communion, the more resplendent will be our heavenly glory; each Communion will increase the splendor of our crown.

— ST. PETER JULIAN EYMARD

Jesus, joy of angels, have mercy on us!

August 3

I understand that, each time we contemplate with desire and devotion the Host in which is hidden Christ's Eucharistic Body, we increase our merits in heaven and secure special joys to be ours later in the beatific vision of God.

— ST. GERTRUDE

Eucharistic Heart of Jesus, unknown by men, I adore thee!

August 4

Holy Communion and offering the Holy Sacrifice are the two most powerful means of intercession for others' conversion.

— ST. JOHN VIANNEY

Blessed be Jesus in the Most Holy Sacrament of the altar!

August 5

My Jesus, teach me how to love. Teach me to use each sacramental union with you as a preparation for the next, so that when my last Holy Communion comes I may but exchange one heaven for another, the heaven of you in my heart for the heaven in which I shall see you in all your beauty face-to-face.

— BLESSED BASIL MOREAU

All you Holy Patriarchs and Prophets, pray for us!

August 6

So they said to him, "Then what sign do you do, that we may see, and believe you? What work do you perform? Our fathers ate manna in the wilderness; as it is written, 'He gave them bread from heaven to eat.' Jesus said to them, "Truly, truly, I say to you, it was not Moses who gave you the bread from heaven; my Father gives you the true bread from heaven. For the bread of God is that which comes down from heaven, and gives life to the world." They said to him, "Lord, give us this bread always." Jesus said to them, "I am the bread of life; he who comes to me shall not hunger, and he who believes in me shall never thirst."

— JOHN 6:30-35

*Heart of Jesus, in whom the Father is well pleased,
have mercy on us!*

August 7

Our Lord has bequeathed to us his Body and Blood under the form of substances in which a multitude of things have been reduced to unity, for one of them, namely bread, consisting as it does of many grains is yet one, and the other, that is to say wine, has its unity of being from the confluent juice of many grapes.

— St. Thomas Aquinas

All glory, honor and praise be to Jesus Crucified!

August 8

Take Communion daily, pushing aside irrational doubts at all times. Trust in joyful blind obedience, and do not fear any evil.

— St. Padre Pio

Most Precious Blood of Jesus Christ,
save us and the whole world!

August 9

What is it we are asking here, O God? We are asking, both for today itself, and the whole of life (a life that in reality is no longer than a day) for that bread which is more precious than anything else; that is, our supernatural bread, the only bread we really need, the only bread absolutely necessary to us if we are to reach our goal — the necessary bread of grace.

— ST. CHARLES DE FOUCAULD

Jesus, pattern of patience, have mercy on us!

August 10

It is at the foot of the altar that we find the strength we need in our isolation. Without the Blessed Sacrament, a situation like mine would not be sustainable. But with the Lord at my side, well then! I continue to always be happy and content. With this gaiety of heart and a smile on my lips, I work with zeal for the good of the poor unfortunate lepers, and little by little, without much fuss, good is done.

— ST. DAMIEN OF MOLOKAI

You who command me to love thee, I love thee, my God!

August 11

He made himself this Bread of Life to satisfy our hunger for this love. And as if that were not enough, he made himself the hungry one, the naked one, the humblest one so that you and I can satisfy his hunger for our human love.

— ST. TERESA OF CALCUTTA

God is our rock of refuge: let us give thanks and praise!

August 12

The most ardent activity will accomplish nothing of value if it forgets for a moment that its main object is to establish the reign of the Eucharist in all hearts.

— SERVANT OF GOD FRANK DUFF

From the spirit of uncleanness, Lord, save your people!

August 13

The Body of Christ is meant to be eaten by the faithful, not to be treated with irreverence.

— ST. HIPPOLYTUS

Jesus, treasure of the faithful, have mercy on us!

August 14

If it is true, as we are bound to believe, that in virtue of the Blessed Sacrament which we receive, our bodies will come to life again on the day of judgment (John 6:55), how could we doubt that Our Lord raised up to heaven, in body and soul, the glorious St. Joseph? For he had the honor and the grace of carrying him so often in his blessed arms, those arms in which Our Lord took so much pleasure.

— St. Francis de Sales

Jesus, abiding in your fullness, Body, Blood, Soul and Divinity, have mercy on us!

August 15

Lord Jesus, how sweet are thy tabernacles!

— St. Louis de Montfort

Blessed be her glorious Assumption!

August 16

Why is he in the tabernacle, forgotten, abandoned, despised?
Doubtless because he loves, but also because he is loved. I
believe that the day on which the earth would lack a heart
beating for Jesus, he would abandon the world, taking away
his doctrine and his love, taking away his Eucharist. But
the earth will never be so lacking. Until the end of time the
Church is there detaining Christ upon the earth with the
bonds of her immortal love.

— SERVANT OF GOD LUIS MARTINEZ

Sacred Host, in which the soul is filled with grace,
have mercy on us!

August 17

Jesus raised the chalice by its two handles to a level with his face, and pronounced the words of consecration. While doing so, he appeared wholly transfigured, as it were transparent, and as though entirely passing into what he was going to give his apostles.

— BLESSED ANNE CATHERINE EMMERICH

Blood of Christ, peace and tenderness of hearts, save us!

August 18

To awaken new devotion to Jesus in the Sacrament of his love, let us often go back in thought to the institution of this sweetest of the sacraments.

— BLESSED BASIL MOREAU

From all sin, Lord, save your people!

August 19

The Blessed Sacrament should be honored by hearing Mass, receiving Communion frequently, visiting the Blessed Sacrament, and making spiritual communions.

— ST. ANTHONY MARY CLARET

Sacred Heart of Jesus, mayest thou be known,
loved and imitated!

August 20

The Holy Eucharist is the wine that germinates virgins.

— BLESSED JAMES ALBERIONE

Hidden God and Savior, have mercy on us!

August 21

Devotion to the Eucharist is the noblest of devotions, because it has God as its object. It is the most profitable for salvation, because it gives us the author of grace. It is the sweetest, because the Lord is sweetness itself.

— St. Pope Pius X

Sacred Host, sign and cause of the unity of the Church, have mercy on us!

August 22

Today I felt the nearness of my mother, my heavenly Mother, although before every Holy Communion I earnestly ask the Mother of God to help me prepare my soul for the coming of her son, and I clearly feel her protection over me. I entreat her to be so gracious as to enkindle in me the fire of God's love, such as burned in her own pure heart at the time of the Incarnation of the Word of God.

— St. Faustina Kowalska

By the mystery of your incarnation Jesus, save your people!

August 23

When you have received our Lord, since he really dwells within you, try to shut the eyes of your body and open those of your soul; look into your heart.

— ST. TERESA OF ÁVILA

From every occasion of sin, O Lord, deliver us!

August 24

As you are a prisoner in the tabernacle, and I, according to your will, am a prisoner in my bed, we can keep each other company.

— BLESSED ALEXANDRINA DA COSTA

Blood of Christ, solace in sorrow, save us!

August 25

At Mass God offers himself as a sacrifice, and when God sacrifices himself, kings should kneel on the floor.

— St. Louis IX, King of France

Jesus, really, truly and substantially present in the Blessed Sacrament, have mercy on us!

August 26

If you are sinful, repent so that you can communicate often. If you are imperfect, go often to Communion that you may amend your faults.

— St. Claude de la Colombière

Heart of Jesus, generous to all who turn to you, have mercy on us!

August 27

I ask only this of you, that you remember me at the altar of the Lord, where ever you may be.

— ST. MONICA TO ST. AUGUSTINE

Thanks be to you, O Lord!

August 28

It was in his flesh that Christ walked among us and it is his flesh that he has given us to eat for our salvation; but no one eats of this flesh without having first adored it, and not only do we not sin in thus adoring it, but we would be sinning if we did not do so.

— ST. AUGUSTINE OF HIPPO

From every sin, Jesus, save your people!

August 29

After Communion the Lord dispenses his graces most
abundantly.

— St. Alphonsus Liguori

*Lamb of God, you take away the sins of the world,
have mercy on us!*

August 30

The heavenly sacrifice, instituted by Christ, is the most
gracious legacy of his new covenant. On the night he was
delivered up to be crucified he left us this gift as a pledge
of his abiding presence. This sacrifice is our sustenance
on life's journey; by it we are nourished and supported
along the road of life until we depart from this world and
make our way to the Lord.

— St. Gaudentius of Brescia

Deliver our souls from eternal damnation, Jesus!

August 31

After receiving Holy Communion I feel a tremendous
heat in my breast.

— VENERABLE PRAXEDES FERNANDEZ

Jesus, victim! I wish to unite myself with thee!

SEPTEMBER

September 1

Exposition is the form of worship our time needs. It is
necessary in order to save society. Society is killing itself,
because it no longer has a center of gravity and charity.
There is no more family life: everyone isolates himself,
concentrates on himself, wants to suffice unto himself.
Disintegration is imminent. But society will be born
again, full of vigor, when all its members come and join
together around our Emmanuel.

— St. Peter Julian Eymard

With all my strength, I love thee, my God!

September 2

Participation [in the Eucharist] is spoken of, because through the Eucharist we participate in the divinity of Jesus. Communion is likewise spoken of, and it is real communion, because through the Eucharist we have communion with Christ and share in his flesh and his divinity.

— St. John Damascene

Let us cry out in praise: my Lord and my God! Alleluia!

September 3

Since his death was the reason of his coming, he now instituted for his apostles and posterity a memorial action of his redemption, which he promised when he said that he was the Bread of Life.

— Venerable Fulton J. Sheen

O saving Victim, have mercy on us!

September 4

If souls understood what treasure they possess in the divine Eucharist, it would be necessary to protect tabernacles with impregnable ramparts; because in the delirium of a holy and devouring hunger, they would go themselves to feed on the Manna of the Seraphim. Churches, at night as in daytime, would overflow with worshipers wasting away with love for the august prisoner.

— BLESSED DINA BELANGER

For those who are indifferent to the Sacrament of your love, have mercy, O Lord!

September 5

When we look at the Cross, we know how much Jesus loved us. When we look at the tabernacle, we know how much Jesus loves us now.

— ST. TERESA OF CALCUTTA

Sacred Host, greatest aid to holiness, have mercy on us!

September 6

Anyone who has a special devotion to the Sacred Eucharist and who tries to repay Christ's infinite love for us with an eager and unselfish love of his own, will experience and fully understand — and this will bring great delight and benefit to his soul — just how precious is a life hidden with Christ in God and just how worthwhile it is to carry on a conversation with Christ, for there is nothing more consoling here on earth, nothing more efficacious for progress along the paths of holiness.

— POPE ST. PAUL VI

Heart of Jesus, infinite in majesty, have mercy on us!

September 7

The Eucharist is the infinite good. For in that Sacrament is Jesus himself, as much present as he was in his home in Nazareth or in the Upper Room at Jerusalem.

— SERVANT OF GOD FRANK DUFF

Jesus, dawn of justice, have mercy on us!

September 8

Mary brings us the Bread of Life. From the day of her birth we salute her as the aurora of the Eucharist, for we know that the Savior of mankind will take from her the substance of that Body and Blood which he will give us in the Adorable Sacrament of his love.

— St. Peter Julian Eymard

Blessed be the great Mother of God, Mary most holy!

September 9

Eternal happiness begins now for the Christian who is comforted with the definitive manna of the Eucharist.

— St. Josemaria Escrivá

All for thee, Most Sacred Heart of Jesus!

September 10

What happiness do we not feel in the presence of God,
when we are alone at his feet before the Sacred Tabernacle!
Redouble your fervor; you are alone to adore your God;
his eyes rest upon you alone.

— St. John Vianney

Heart of Jesus, source of all consolation, have mercy on us!

September 11

Without Communion, one is constantly in the heat of battle.
Receive Communion therefore! Eat the Bread of Life if you
wish to live well, if you wish to obtain sufficient strength for
the Christian combat, if you wish to possess happiness even
in the thick of misfortune.

— St. Peter Julian Eymard

*Lamb of God, who takes away the sins of the world, graciously
hear us, O Lord!*

September 12

Aware of the great blessing contained therein for all men, Mary foresaw also the ingratitude of mortals in regard to this ineffable Sacrament, established for their benefit, and she resolved to atone, with all the powers of her being, for our shameless and ungrateful behavior. She took upon herself the duty of rendering thanks to the eternal Father and to his divine Son for this extraordinary and wonderful benefit to the human race.

— VENERABLE MARY OF AGREDA

Blessed be the name of Mary, Virgin and Mother!

September 13

The virtue of gratitude obliges us to make reparation, insofar as we can, for the shameful treatment received by the Body of the Savior.

— BLESSED BASIL MOREAU

Jesus, Victim! I wish to immolate myself with thee!

September 14

Let us submit to God in all things and not contradict him, even if what he says seems to contradict our reason and intellect; let his word prevail over our reason and intellect. Let us act in this way with regard to the Eucharistic mysteries, and not limit our attention just to what can be perceived by the senses, but instead hold fast to his words. For his word cannot deceive.

— ST. JOHN CHRYSOSTOM

*Heart of Jesus, salvation of all who trust in you,
have mercy on us!*

September 15

Oh, my Lord, it seems to me that if I were dead, I should come to life in order to receive thee, and if an unconsecrated host were given to me, that I should know it by the taste, as one knows wine from water.

— ST. CATHERINE OF GENOA

*Jesus, with us always until the end of the world,
have mercy on us!*

September 16

The Lord's sacrifices proclaim the unity of Christians who are bound together by a firm and unshakeable charity. For when the Lord calls the bread that has been made from many grains of wheat his Body, he is describing our people whose unity he has sustained; and when he refers to wine pressed from many grapes and berries as his Blood, once again he is speaking of our flock which has been formed by fusing many into one.

— ST. CYPRIAN

Heart of Jesus, our peace and reconciliation, have mercy on us!

September 17

Jesus hides in the Blessed Sacrament of the altar because he wants us to dare to approach him. He wants to nourish us so we become one single thing with him.

— ST. JOSEMARIA ESCRIVÁ

O Lord, grant salvation!

September 18

Humility, obedience, meekness, and love are the virtues that shine through the Cross and the Blessed Sacrament of the Altar.

— St. Anthony Mary Claret

Jesus, hidden under the appearance of bread, have mercy on us!

September 19

That genuine charity which knows how to do and to suffer all things for the salvation and the benefit of all, leaps forth with all the heat and energy of a flame from that most holy Eucharist in which Christ himself is present and lives, in which he indulges to the utmost.

— Pope Leo XIII

Bread made flesh by the omnipotence of the Word, have mercy on us!

September 20

Wherever the sacred Host is to be found, there is the living God, there is your Savior, as really as when he was living and talking in Galilee and Judea, as really as he now is in heaven.

— St. Charles de Foucauld

The noble fellowship of prophets praise you!

September 21

Let us love this Lord who has found a way to penetrate the wall of flesh that is usually an obstacle between human hearts. Only God could have devised so sweet a way of enabling the loving soul to contract an actual union with the beloved, and yet, this union that he meant for all is realized by such a comparatively small number. Let us make up to him for all those into whose hearts he can never come in his humanity. Let us adore him now and forever, not only for Catholics who do not adore him, but also to supply the place of all – heretics, schismatics, infidels, atheists, blasphemers, Muslims, Jews, and idolaters who do not adore him.

— BLESSED BASIL MOREAU

Holy Eucharist, hope of despairing souls, save us!

September 22

The piety of the Christian people has always very rightly sensed a profound link between devotion to the Blessed Virgin and worship of the Eucharist. Mary guides the faithful to the Eucharist.

— POPE ST. JOHN PAUL II

You are seated at God's right hand in glory!

September 23

Because of a food, we were cast out of the loveliness of paradise, but by means of another food we have been restored to the joys of paradise. Eve ate the food by which she condemned us to the hunger of an eternal fast. Mary brought forth the food that opened for us the entrance to the banquet of heaven.

— ST. PETER DAMIAN

Sacred Host, in which we are given a pledge of future glory, have mercy on us!

September 24

Let us speak to the purpose and beseech the Father to give us grace so to prepare ourselves for the reception of this sacred and heavenly food that, although our bodily eyes cannot rejoice in looking on Jesus, hidden as he is beneath the sacramental veils, yet he may reveal himself to the sight of our soul and may teach us that this Bread is a special kind of nutriment, which contains in itself sweetness and joy, and sustains our life.

— ST. TERESA OF ÁVILA

Jesus, make our hearts like unto thine!

September 25

At the sight of a steeple you can say, what's that in there? The Body of our Lord. Why is he there? Because a priest has said Holy Mass.

— ST. JOHN VIANNEY

Lord of all, we bow before thee!

September 26

The Lord is immolated in an unbloody way in the Sacrifice of the Mass and he re-presents the sacrifice of the Cross and applies its salvific power at the moment when he becomes sacramentally present — through the words of consecration — as the spiritual food of the faithful, under the appearances of bread and wine.

— POPE ST. PAUL VI

Heart of Jesus, pierced by a lance, have mercy on us!

September 27

When you have received Jesus into your hearts, can any sacrifice be impossible for you?

— ST. VINCENT DE PAUL

Sacred Host, bond of charity, have mercy on us!

September 28

Jesus in the Blessed Sacrament is the most tender of friends with souls that seek to please him. His goodness knows how to proportion itself to the littlest of his creatures as to the greatest. Do not fear, then, in solitary conversations, to speak to him of your woes, your fears, your troubles, those who are dear to you, your plans, your hopes; do it confidently and with an open heart.

— St. Damien of Molokai

With all my heart, I love thee, my God!

September 29

It is easier for the world to survive without the sun than without the Holy Sacrifice of the Mass.

— St. Padre Pio

*Precious Blood of Jesus Christ,
the Christian's true faith, set us free!*

September 30

It is in our churches, in this tabernacle, that the living Body of the Savior rests. He was but nine months in the womb of Mary, three hours on the cross, three days in the tomb. Yet he is always in our churches. This is why they do not empty of angels, archangels, and seraphim unceasingly adoring him.

— ST. CLAUDE DE LA COLOMBIÈRE

Above all possessions and honor, I love thee, my God!

OCTOBER

October 1

From her [Mary's] own womb's immaculate flesh she
gave birth to the nutriment of our souls.

— ST. PETER DAMIAN

Heart of Jesus, king and center of all hearts, have mercy on us!

October 2

The Eucharist is a fire which inflames us, that, like lions
breathing fire, we may retire from the altar being made
terrible to the Devil.

— ST. JOHN CHRYSOSTOM

From the snares of the devil, Lord, save your people!

October 3

The greatest love story of all time is contained in a
tiny white host.

— VENERABLE FULTON J. SHEEN

Lord, be merciful. Jesus, save your people!

October 4

Adoration is prayer that prolongs the celebration and the
Eucharistic communion and in which the soul continues
to be nourished: it is nourished with love, truth, peace; it
is nourished with hope, because the one before whom we
prostrate ourselves does not judge us, does not crush us but
liberates and transforms us.

— POPE BENEDICT XVI

With all my soul, I love thee, my God!

October 5

The most solemn moment of my life is the moment when I receive Holy Communion. I long for each Holy Communion, and for every Holy Communion I give thanks to the Most Holy Trinity. If the angels were capable of envy, they would envy us for two things; one is the receiving of Holy Communion, and the other is suffering.

— St. Faustina Kowalska

St. Faustina, secretary of Divine Mercy, pray for us!

October 6

The rosary is a great test of faith. What the Eucharist
is in the order of sacraments, that the rosary is in order
of sacramentals — the mystery and the test of faith, the
touchstone by which the soul is judged in its humility.
The mark of the Christian is the willingness to look for
the Divine in the flesh of a babe in a crib, the continuing
Christ under the appearance of bread on an altar, and a
meditation and a prayer on a string of beads.

— VENERABLE FULTON J. SHEEN

This is the day the Lord has made, let us be glad and rejoice in it!

October 7

The rosary, in a gentle, subtle way leads one to the Eucharist,
to the Most Blessed Sacrament: those who approach Jesus in
thought, yearn to approach him in reality; those who know
Jesus cannot but love him; indeed, those who truly love Jesus
cannot forego possessing him.

— BLESSED BARTOLO LONGO

Our Lady of the Rosary, pray for us!

October 8

When we are before the Blessed Sacrament, let us open our heart; our good God will open his. We shall go to him; he will come to us; the one to ask, the other to receive. It will be like a breath from one to the other.

— St. John Vianney

Heart of Jesus, patient and full of mercy, have mercy on us!

October 9

The flesh of Christ is the flesh of Mary, and although it was raised to great glory in his Resurrection, yet it still remained the same that was taken from Mary.

— St. Augustine

I love and adore thee, my God!

October 10

By the Eucharistic celebration we already unite ourselves with the heavenly liturgy and anticipate eternal life, when God will be all in all.

— CATECHISM OF THE CATHOLIC CHURCH

From the desire of being preferred to others, deliver me, Jesus!

October 11

Every time I hear anyone speak of the Sacred Heart of Jesus or of the Blessed Sacrament, I feel an indescribable joy. It is as if a wave of precious memories, sweet affections and joyful hopes swept over my poor person, making me tremble with happiness and filling my soul with tenderness. These are loving appeals from Jesus, who wants me whole heartedly there, at the source of all goodness, his Sacred Heart, throbbing mysteriously behind the Eucharistic veils.

— POPE ST. JOHN XXIII

That we may see you one day face to face in heaven, we beseech you, hear us!

October 12

Since we who are in the flesh have Christ dwelling in us through his flesh, we shall draw life from him in the same way as he draws life from the Father.

— St. Hilary

Raise our minds to desire the things of heaven, Lord!

October 13

Devotion to our Lord Jesus Christ and devotion to Mary are intimately united. The more we love Jesus Christ in the Blessed Sacrament, the more we love the Blessed Virgin; and the more we love the Blessed Virgin, the more we love the Blessed Sacrament.

— St. Mary Euphrasia Pelletier

Jesus, splendor of the Father, have mercy on us!

October 14

After the Holy Liturgy of the Eucharist, the prayer
of the rosary is what better draws to our spirit the
mysteries of Faith, Hope and Charity. The rosary is the
spiritual bread of souls.

— SERVANT OF GOD LÚCIA DOS SANTOS

*That it may please you to bring us to true penance, Lord,
hear our prayer!*

October 15

Do you not know that this most holy Sacrament is a most
beneficial food even for our body and a powerful remedy
for its diseases? I am sure that it is. I am acquainted with a
person subject to severe illness which often cause her acute
pain; she was freed from them instantaneously by this Bread,
and remained in perfect health.

— ST. TERESA OF ÁVILA

Sacred Host, spiritual food, have mercy on us!

October 16

I promise thee, in the excessive mercy of my heart, that my all-powerful love will grant to all those who communicate (receive Holy Communion) on the First Friday of the month, for nine consecutive months, the grace of final penitence; they shall not die in my displeasure nor without the Sacraments; my Divine Heart shall be their refuge in this last moment.

— JESUS TO ST. MARGARET MARY ALACOQUE

Most Sacred Heart of Jesus, have mercy on us!

October 17

For me the tabernacle has always been a Bethany, a quiet and pleasant place where Christ resides. A place where we can tell him about our worries, our sufferings, our desires, our joys, with the same sort of simplicity and naturalness as Martha, Mary, and Lazarus. That is why I rejoice when I come across a church — even if I can only see the silhouette in the distance — as I make my way through the streets of an unfamiliar town or city; it's another tabernacle, another opportunity for the soul to escape and join our Lord in the Sacrament.

— ST. JOSEMARIA ESCRIVÁ

From the desire of being loved, deliver me, Jesus!

October 18

And he took bread, and when he had given thanks he broke it and gave it to them, saying, "This is my body which is given for you. Do this in remembrance of me." And likewise the chalice after supper, saying, "This chalice which is poured out for you is the new covenant in my blood."

— LUKE 22: 15-20

St. Luke the Evangelist, pray for us!

October 19

When I am before the Blessed Sacrament, I feel such a lively faith that I can't describe it. Christ in the Eucharist is almost tangible to me.

— ST. ANTHONY MARY CLARET

Perpetual sacrifice, have mercy on us!

October 20

Our Lord in the Blessed Sacrament has his hands full of graces, and he is ready to bestow them on anyone who asks for them.

— St. Peter of Alcantara

Sacred Host, in which we partake of Christ, have mercy on us!

October 21

You see how efficacious are the words of Christ. If the word of the Lord Jesus is so powerful as to summon into existence that which did not exist, namely the world, how much more powerful is his word to change into something else that which already has existence?

— St. Ambrose

Sacred Heart of Jesus, I believe in thy love for me!

October 22

The Church draws her life from the Eucharist. This truth does not simply express a daily experience of faith, but recapitulates the heart of the mystery of the Church.

— POPE ST. JOHN PAUL II

St. John Paul II, Apostle of the Eucharist, pray for us!

October 23

God bless the one who made Jesus come down from heaven and gave him to me!

— ST. HEDWIG

Jesus, divine Victim on the altar for our salvation, have mercy on us!

October 24

The heavenly Sacrifice, instituted by Christ, is the most gracious legacy of his new covenant. On the night he was delivered up to be crucified, he left us this gift as a pledge of his abiding presence.

— ST. GAUDENTIUS OF BRESCIA

That we may never neglect to thank you for so wonderful a blessing, we beseech you, hear us!

October 25

In order to satisfy his love, he instituted the sacrament of the Holy Eucharist and went to the extent of changing and overturning nature itself.

— ST. LOUIS DE MONTFORT

By your hidden life, Jesus, save your people!

October 26

In Communion, you have the happiness of possessing Jesus Christ in your heart, where he is Body and Soul, as he was on earth during his mortal life.

— ST. JOHN VIANNEY

Heart of Jesus, in whom there dwells the fullness of God, have mercy on us!

October 27

He called the bread his living body and filled it with himself and his Spirit. He who eats it with faith, eats fire and spirit.

— ST. EPHREM

God the Holy Spirit, have mercy on us!

October 28

In the presence of the Adorable Host, it is faith that will capture our imagination and our thoughts, and will hold all the powers of soul and body respectfully submissive, fixed, and almost totally subdued.

— BLESSED BASIL MOREAU

Saints Simon and Jude, pray for us!

October 29

Communion gives us perseverance to the end. Nothing is so discouraging as a long road ahead of us, and it is the common feeling of beginners to say "I can never hold out so long!" If you wish final perseverance, receive our Lord!

— ST. PETER JULIAN EYMARD

Heart of Jesus, obedient even to death, have mercy on us!

October 30

Through your love for the Eucharist, you will also rediscover the Sacrament of Reconciliation, in which the merciful goodness of God always allows us to make a fresh start in our lives.

— POPE BENEDICT XVI

Redeemer of the world, have mercy on us!

October 31

Let weak and frail man come here in humble entreaty to adore the Sacrament of Christ, not to discuss high things, or to wish to penetrate difficulties, but to bow down to secret things in humble veneration.

— ST. PAUL OF THE CROSS

That we may celebrate the Holy Sacrifice of the Mass in accordance with its sublime dignity, we beseech you, hear us!

NOVEMBER

November 1

It is our very sweet duty to honor and adore in the blessed Host which our eyes see, the Incarnate Word whom they cannot see, and who, without leaving heaven, is made present before us.

— POPE ST. PAUL VI

Heart of Jesus, delight of all the saints have, mercy on us!

November 2

You remain upon this miserable world in the Most Holy and exceedingly admirable Sacrament of the altar, and now you come to me and unite yourself intimately to me as nourishment.

— ST. MAXIMILIAN KOLBE

Glory to the Father, and to the Son, and to the Holy Spirit!

November 3

A Sacrament so great and so rich in all manner of blessings can never be extolled as it deserves by human eloquence, nor adequately venerated by the worship of man.

— POPE LEO XIII

Unbloody sacrifice, have mercy on us!

November 4

A man who fails to love the Mass fails to love Christ. We must make an effort to live the Mass with calm and serenity, with devotion and affection. Those who love acquire a finesse, a sensitivity of soul that makes them notice details that are sometimes very small, but that are important because they express the love of a passionate heart. This is how we should attend Holy Mass. And this is why I have always suspected that those who want the Mass to be over quickly show, with this insensitive attitude, that they have not yet realized what the sacrifice of the altar means.

— ST. JOSEMARIA ESCRIVÁ

Above all pleasures and delights, I love thee, my God!

November 5

To believe in love is everything. It is not enough to believe in truth. We must believe in love, and love is our Lord in the Blessed Sacrament.

— St. Peter Julian Eymard

From all spiritual dangers, Lord, deliver your people!

November 6

The Holy Eucharist is the final effort of love which seeks to give itself; it is the prodigy of omnipotence in the service of infinite charity.

— Blessed Columba Marmion

O Lord, grant us salvation!

November 7

If we meditated on the most holy Sacrament of the Eucharist we would not only hear his heartbeats, we would hear our hearts beating in union with his.

— SERVANT OF GOD CATHERINE DOHERTY

Heart of Jesus, our life and resurrection, have mercy on us!

November 8

When you visit the Most Blessed Sacrament, approach Jesus with the love of the Blessed Virgin, St. Joseph, and St. John.

— ST. JOSEPH SEBASTIAN PELCZAR

Jesus, mighty God, have mercy on us!

November 9

When you hear Mass, but do not go to Holy Communion, you may make an act of Spiritual Communion, which is exceedingly profitable. Recollect yourselves in the same manner: this impresses a deep love for our Lord on our minds; for if we prepare our souls to receive him, he never fails, in many ways unknown to us, to give us his grace.

— ST. TERESA OF ÁVILA

On souls beset by temptation, have mercy!

November 10

One cannot separate the most Holy Eucharist from the Passion of Jesus.

— ST. ANDRE OF AVELLINO

Precious Blood of Jesus Christ, Foundation of the Christian Faith, set us free!

November 11

I wish to add something that is clearly awe inspiring, but do not be surprised or upset. What is this? It is the same offering, no matter who offers it, be it Peter or Paul. It is the same one that Christ gave to his disciples and the same one that priests now perform: the latter is in no way inferior to the former, for it is not men who sanctify the latter, but he who sanctified the former. For just as the words which God spoke are the same as those that the priest now pronounces, so too the offering is the same.

— ST. JOHN CHRYSOSTOM

Jesus, crown of all saints, have mercy on us!

November 12

Go to the church and give my love to the Hidden Jesus.

— ST. FRANCISCO MARTO

By your childhood, Jesus, save your people!

November 13

My dear angel, go there [to visit Jesus in the Blessed Sacrament] for me.

— St. Stanislaus Kostka

Jesus, Bread of angels, have mercy on us!

November 14

Understand that the strength by which you bear sufferings comes from frequent Communions. So approach this fountain of mercy often, to draw with the vessel of trust whatever you need.

— Jesus to St. Faustina Kowalska

Jesus, I trust in you!

November 15

I adore you, Blood of the new and eternal Testament,
flowing from the veins of Jesus in Gethsemane, from the
flesh torn by scourges in the Praetorium, from his pierced
hands and feet and from his opened side on Golgotha. I
adore you in the Sacraments, in the Eucharist, where I know
you are substantially present.

— St. Albert the Great

Living bread that came down from heaven, have mercy on us!

November 16

I ask nothing more of thee than thou come to receive me
with a heart divested of thyself.

— Jesus to St. Gertrude

Jesus, Prince of Peace, have mercy on us!

November 17

We must beg for good adorers; the Blessed Sacrament needs them to replace St. Joseph and to imitate his life of adoration.

— St. Peter Julian Eymard

*Eucharistic Heart of Jesus, wishing to be with souls,
I adore thee!*

November 18

When you cannot have the blessing of actual Communion, at least communicate in heart and mind, uniting yourself by ardent desire to the life-giving Body of the Savior.

— St. Francis de Sales

Heavenly antidote against the poison of sin, have mercy on us!

November 19

O Sacred Host, fountain of divine sweetness, you give strength to my soul; you are the Omnipotent One, who took flesh of the Virgin. You come to my heart, in secret, beyond reach of the groping senses.

— ST. FAUSTINA KOWALSKA

Jesus, our refuge, have mercy on us!

November 20

That Jesus whom others admire, Catholics possess — ever living in the Eucharist. They have free access to him and can, and should, receive him even daily as the food of their souls.

— SERVANT OF GOD FRANK DUFF

Above all created things in Heaven or on earth, I love thee, my God!

November 21

O my daughter! Would that the believers in the holy Catholic faith opened their hardened and stony hearts in order to attain to a true understanding of the sacred and mysterious blessing of the Holy Eucharist! If they would only detach themselves, root out and reject their earthly inclinations, and, restraining their passions, apply themselves with living faith to study by the divine light their great happiness in thus possessing their eternal God in the holy Sacrament and in being able, by its reception, to participate in the full effects of this heavenly manna!

— MARY TO VENERABLE MARY OF AGREDA

Jesus, Son of the Virgin Mary, have mercy on us!

November 22

I cannot conceive how anyone can keep his purity in the world or progress at all without Communion.

— ST. PETER JULIAN EYMARD

Jesus, courage of martyrs, have mercy on us!

November 23

The Eucharist is the secret of my day. It gives strength and meaning to all my activities of service to the Church and to the whole world.

— POPE ST. JOHN PAUL II

The Lord is God, and he has given us light!

November 24

Man fell by means of the food of the death-giving tree; man is raised up by means of the life-giving tree. On the former hung the food of death, on the latter the nourishment of life. Eating of the former earned a wound; the taste of this latter restored health. Eating wounded us, eating healed us.

— POPE URBAN IV

Only for thyself, I love thee, my God!

November 25

Today there are many who are trying to tone down on the Eucharist on which the Mass depends. The idea at work is to propitiate the Protestants, to devise a formula which they would accept. That must obviously mean that we have to give away to some extent so as to meet them. But how can we abandon one inch of ground in regard to the Eucharist? It is either the Real Presence of Jesus or it ceases to be that.

— SERVANT OF GOD FRANK DUFF

In prosperity and adversity, I love thee, my God!

November 26

Jesus is not an idea, a sentiment, a memory! Jesus is a person, always alive and present with us! Love Jesus present in the Eucharist. He is present in a sacrificial way in Holy Mass, which renews the sacrifice of the Cross. To go to Mass means going to Calvary to meet him, our Redeemer. He comes to us in Holy Communion and remains present in the tabernacles of our churches, for he is our friend.

— POPE ST. JOHN PAUL II

Heart of Jesus, worthy of all praise, have mercy on us!

November 27

We faithfully confess, that before the consecration it is bread and wine, the product of nature; but after consecration it is the Body and Blood of Christ, consecrated by the blessing.

— ST. AUGUSTINE OF HIPPO

Sweet Heart of my Jesus, grant that I may ever love thee more!

November 28

There was an indescribable solemnity and order in all the actions of Jesus during the institution of the Holy Eucharist, and his every movement was most majestic.

— BLESSED ANNE CATHERINE EMMERICH

Jesus, teacher of the apostles, have mercy on us!

November 29

Mary adored Jesus present in the Most Blessed Sacrament. Mary received the Holy Eucharist. Mary assisted at Mass celebrated by the Apostles. How can we measure Mary's depth of thought, her most holy and intense love, her intimacy of union with the Eucharistic Jesus? It is impossible for us to do so. Mary was an adorer of the Holy Eucharist even more than she had been an adorer in the stable. From the Eucharistic Jesus Mary learned more than she had learned at Nazareth.

— BLESSED JAMES ALBERIONE

Blessed be the Eternal Love!

November 30

We must spare no pains in our care of the ciborium and of the tabernacle, and we must be watchful for the cleanliness of the sacred buildings.

— BLESSED COLUMBA MARMION

Because thou art infinitely perfect, I love thee, my God!

DECEMBER

December 1

People talk about Lazarus who had the joy of entertaining the Divine Savior in his home; but Lazarus only had him by his side, while we, if we will, may have him in our heart just as often as we wish.

— St. John Vianney

Heart of Jesus, hope of all who die in you, have mercy on us!

December 2

Go and stay for a little while near the Hidden Jesus.

— St. Francisco Marto

From everlasting death, Lord, save your people!

December 3

In the Eucharist he has made himself our support and
company on our pilgrim way.

— ST. IGNATIUS LOYOLA

Because thou are infinitely worthy of being loved,
I love thee, my God!

December 4

Behold, I am with you always, to the close of the age.

— MATTHEW 28: 20

Only-begotten Son of the Eternal Father, save us!

December 5

This is an undeniable fact: Marian souls are and become Eucharistic souls and Eucharistic souls are and become Marian souls.

— BLESSED GABRIEL ALLEGRA

Jesus, infinite goodness, have mercy on us!

December 6

For as the bread, which is produced from the earth, when it receives the invocation of God, is no longer common bread, but the Eucharist, consisting of two realities, earthly and heavenly; so also our bodies, when they receive the Eucharist, are no longer corruptible, having the hope of resurrection to eternity.

— ST. IRENAEUS

In life and in death, I love thee, my God!

December 7

One single Holy Communion is enough to make one holy. It all depends on the inner dispositions, on preparation.

— St. Maximilian Kolbe

Jesus, the true light, have mercy on us!

December 8

The Eucharist produces impulses of angelic love and has the singular capacity of effecting in souls a holy, instinctive tenderness for the Queen of Angels. She has given us flesh of her flesh and bone of her bone, and in the Eucharist she continues to give us this sweet, virginal, heavenly food.

— St. Albert the Great

Blessed be her holy and Immaculate Conception!

December 9

Do you want the Lord to give you many graces? Visit him often. Do you want him to give you few graces? Visit him rarely. Do you want the devil to attack you? Visit Jesus rarely in the Blessed Sacrament. Do you want him to flee from you? Visit Jesus often. Do you want to conquer the devil? Take refuge often at the feet of Jesus. Dear ones, the visit to the Blessed Sacrament is an extremely necessary way to conquer the devil. Therefore, go often to visit Jesus and the devil will not come out victorious against you.

— ST. JOHN BOSCO

Give us the grace to spend time with you in the Blessed Sacrament!

December 10

The Eucharist began at Bethlehem in Mary's arms. It was she who brought to humanity the Bread for which it was famishing, and which alone can nourish it. She it was who took care of that Bread for us. It was she who nourished the Lamb whose life-giving flesh we feed upon. She nourished him with her virginal milk; she nourished him for the sacrifice, for she foreknew his destiny.

— St. Peter Julian Eymard

Adoration! Adoration! Adoration!

December 11

The Mass is the spiritual food that sustains me — without which I could not get through one single day or hour in my life.

— St. Teresa of Calcutta

Precious Blood of Jesus Christ, poured out for sinners, save us!

December 12

If people see that their priests approach the divine mysteries
with holy fear and trembling, they learn to treat and receive
their God in like manner. Those that so honor him shall
shine in heaven like the sun among the stars.

— Mary to Venerable Mary of Agreda

Blood of Christ, hope of the penitent, save us!

December 13

To leave the tabernacle to go and venerate statues would be
to leave the Jesus living at my side to go into another room
to greet his portrait.

— St. Charles de Foucauld

Lion of the tribe of Judah, save us!

December 14

They have not realized that the least of the benefits which come from this Most Holy Sacrament is that which concerns the senses; and that the invisible part of the grace that it bestows is much greater; for, in order that they may look at it with eyes of faith, God often withholds from them these other consolations and sweetnesses of sense.

— ST. JOHN OF THE CROSS

Wheat of the elect, have mercy on us!

December 15

During Communion I often repeated these words from *The Imitation of Christ*: "O God, who are unutterable sweetness, turn to bitterness for me all the comforts of earth!" The words came effortlessly from my lips. I said them like a child reciting words put into its mind by a beloved friend.

— ST. THÉRÈSE OF LISIEUX

Jesus, purity of virgins, have mercy on us!

December 16

Bear in mind that our Lord never reproaches us in the first moments of Communion. That is the devil troubling our thoughts in order to prevent us from enjoying the sweetness of Jesus. He tries to make our Lord out to be a strict Master, a stern Judge, and, in that way, he frightens us. We are almost persuaded to abandon our thanksgiving in order to escape the eye of vengeance. Oh, that is not our Lord's character!

— St. Peter Julian Eymard

Jesus, Good Shepherd, have mercy on us!

December 17

In a word this Sacrament is, as it were, the very soul of the Church; and to it the grace of the priesthood is ordered and directed in all its fullness and in each of its successive grades.

— Pope Leo XIII

Priest and victim, have mercy on us!

December 18

If while Jesus lived in the world, the mere touch of his garments healed the sick, who can doubt that when he is dwelling in the very center of our being he will work miracles in us if we have a living faith in him? And will he not grant our petitions while he is our guest?

— St. Teresa of Ávila

Help me to strip myself of all vainglory!

December 19

To make room in our life for the Eucharistic Lord, so that he can change our life into his – is that asking too much?

— St. Teresa Benedicta of the Cross

That we may receive you frequently in Holy Communion with real devotion and true humility, we beseech you, hear us!

December 20

Grieve over the contempt cast upon Jesus Christ in the Blessed Sacrament, and try to make amends for it by a greater and more ardent love.

— St. John Vianney

Heart of Jesus, victim of our sins, have mercy on us!

December 21

The mark of the Christian is the willingness to look for the divine in the flesh of a babe in a crib, the continuing Christ under the appearance of bread on an altar.

— Venerable Fulton J. Sheen

Blood of Christ, Incarnate Word of God, save us!

December 22

Saint Joseph went in haste with Mary to Bethlehem which means "house of bread," so that the bread of eternal life might be born there.

— VENERABLE JOSEPH MINDSZENTY

From the desire of being extolled, deliver me, Jesus!

December 23

May the Holy Eucharist and perfect abandonment to God's will be your heaven on earth.

— BLESSED MARY ANNE BLONDIN

*In union with the Blessed Virgin Mary and St. Joseph,
I love thee, my God!*

December 24

So submissive was he to her care that the door that slammed in her face in Bethlehem also slammed on him. If there was no room for her in the inn, then there was no room for him. As she was the ciborium before he was born, so she was his monstrance after Bethlehem. To her fell the happy lot of exposing, in the chapel of a stable, the "Blessed Sacrament," the body, blood, soul, and divinity of Jesus Christ. She enthroned him for adoration before Wise Men and shepherds, before the very simple and the very learned.

— VENERABLE FULTON J. SHEEN

In wealth and in poverty, I love thee, my God!

December 25

You were not nearer to the Blessed Virgin during the nine months she carried you in her womb than you are to me when you rest on my tongue at Holy Communion. You were no closer to the Blessed Virgin and St. Joseph in the caves at Bethlehem or the house at Nazareth or during the flight into Egypt, or at any moment of that divine family life than you are to me at this moment – in the tabernacle. Saint Mary Magdalene was no closer to you when she sat at your feet at Bethany than I am here at the foot of this altar. You were no nearer to your apostles when you were sitting in the midst of them than you are to me now, my God. How blessed I am!

— St. Charles de Foucauld

By your birth, Jesus, save your people!

December 26

Out of the darkness of my life, so much frustrated, I put before you the one great thing to love on earth: the Blessed Sacrament. There you will find romance, glory, honor, fidelity, and the true way of all your loves upon the earth, and more than that: death; by the divine paradox, that which ends life, and demands the surrender of all, and yet by the taste (or foretaste) of which alone can what you seek in your earthly relationships (love, faithfulness, joy) be maintained, or take on that complexion of reality, or eternal endurance, that every man's heart desires.

— J.R.R. TOLKIEN

Because you are all good, I love thee, my God!

December 27

Do not labor for food which perishes, but for food which endures to eternal life, which the Son of man will give to you; for on him has God the Father set his seal. Truly, truly, I say to you, he who believes has eternal life. I am the Bread of Life. I am the living bread which comes down from heaven; if any man eats of this bread, he will live forever; and the bread which I shall give for the life of the world is my flesh.

— JOHN 6: 27, 47-48, 51

St. John, Apostle and Evangelist, pray for us!

December 28

O Jesus, be mindful of your own bitter Passion and do not permit the loss of souls redeemed at so dear a price of your most precious Blood. O Jesus, when I consider the great price of your Blood, I rejoice at its immensity, for one drop alone would have been enough for the salvation of all sinners.

— ST. FAUSTINA KOWALSKA

Blood of Jesus Christ, ocean of mercy, set us free!

December 29

You may be sure that of all the moments in your life, the time you spend before the divine Sacrament will be that which will give you strength during life and more consolation at the hour of your death and during eternity.

— St. Alphonsus Liguori

I beg you, by your Resurrection, make me rise glorious with you on the last day!

December 30

The Eucharist, as Christ's saving presence in the community of the faithful and its spiritual food, is the most precious possession which the Church can have in her journey through history.

— Pope St. John Paul II

My spirit rejoices in God my Savior!

December 31

Are we in affliction? We shall find all manner of consolation at Mass. Are we tempted? Let us hear Holy Mass, and we shall find there a way of overcoming the devil.

— St. John Chrysostom

From plague, famine, and war, Lord, save your people!

PRAYERS

Fátima Prayers

Pardon Prayer

My God, I believe, I adore, I trust, and I love thee! I beg pardon for those who do not believe, do not adore, do not trust, and do not love thee.

The Angel's Prayer

O most Holy Trinity — Father, Son, and Holy Spirit — I adore thee profoundly. I offer thee the most Precious Body, Blood, Soul, and Divinity of Jesus Christ — present in all the tabernacles of the world in reparation for the outrages, sacrileges, and indifference by which he is offended. By the infinite merits of the Sacred Heart of Jesus and the Immaculate Heart of Mary, I beg the conversion of poor sinners.

Eucharistic Prayer

Most Holy Trinity, I adore thee! My God, my God, I love thee in the Most Blessed Sacrament!

Sacrifice Prayer

O my Jesus, it is for love of you, in reparation for the offenses committed against the Immaculate Heart of Mary, and for the conversion of poor sinners.

Act of Spiritual Communion
(by St. Alphonsus Liguori)

My Jesus, I believe that you are present in the Most Holy Sacrament. I love you above all things, and I desire to receive you into my soul. Since I cannot at this moment receive you sacramentally, come at least spiritually into my heart. I embrace you as if you were already there and unite myself wholly to you, never permit me to be separated from you. Amen.

Prayer of Saint Gertrude the Great

Eternal Father, I offer thee the most Precious Blood of thy Divine Son, Jesus, in union with the Masses said throughout the world today, for all the Holy Souls in purgatory, for sinners everywhere, for sinners in the universal church, those in my own home and within my family. Amen.

Prayer for the Souls in Purgatory

O gentle heart of Jesus, ever present in the Blessed Sacrament, ever consumed with burning love for the poor captive souls in Purgatory, have mercy on them. Be not severe in your judgments, but let some drops of your Precious Blood fall upon the devouring flames. And, Merciful Savior, send your angels to conduct them to a place of refreshment, light and peace. Amen.

Anima Christi

Soul of Christ, sanctify me. Body of Christ, save me. Blood of Christ, inebriate me. Water from the side of Christ, wash me. O good Jesus, hear me. Within thy wounds hide me. Permit me not to be separated from thee. From the malignant enemy, defend me. In the hour of my death, call me. And bid me come to thee. That with thy saints I may praise thee, forever and ever. Amen.

Litany of the Blessed Sacrament

Lord, have mercy.
Christ, have mercy.
Lord, have mercy.
God the Father in heaven, *have mercy on us*.
God the Son, Redeemer of the world,
God the Holy Spirit,
Holy Trinity, one God,

Jesus, present with us now in this holy sacrament.
We adore you.
Jesus, who changed water into wine and blessed the
wedding at Cana.
Jesus, who ate with sinners and tax collectors.
Jesus, who blessed the home of Martha and Mary.
Jesus, who sat at table with your friends at the Last Supper.
Jesus, who offered your body on the Cross for all.
Jesus, who blessed and broke bread for Cleopas and
his companion.
Jesus, throned in the highest at the marriage supper
of the Lamb.

Jesus, *have mercy upon us*.
Jesus, Bread of Life.
Jesus, priest of the new covenant.
Jesus, manna from heaven.
Jesus, cup of blessing.
Jesus, food of eternal life.

In the gift of the Eucharist,
we proclaim the Lord's death until he comes again.
In the gift of the Eucharist.
you satisfy our hunger.
In the gift of the Eucharist,
you unite us into one body.

In Communion,
may we receive you worthily.
In Communion,
may we humbly adore you.
In Communion,
may we pledge our lives to serve you.
In Communion,
**may we be strengthened to deeds of love and
compassion**.

Lamb of God, you take away the sin of the world,
have mercy on us.
Lamb of God, you take away the sin of the world,
have mercy on us.
Lamb of God, you take away the sin of the world,
grant us peace.
Jesus said, "I am the bread of life.
Whoever comes to me will never be hungry,
and whoever believes in me will never thirst.'

Lord Jesus, Christ
we thank you that in this wonderful Sacrament
you have given us the memorial of your Passion:
grant us so to reverence the sacred mysteries
of your Body and Blood
that we may know within ourselves
and show forth in our lives the fruits of your redemption;
for you live and reign with the Father
in the unity of the Holy Spirit,
God, forever and forever. **Amen.**

Litany of the Most Precious Blood of Our Lord Jesus Christ

Lord, have mercy on us, *Christ, have mercy on us.*
Lord, have mercy on us, Christ hear us,
Christ graciously hear us.
God our Father in heaven, *Have mercy on us!*
God the Son, Redeemer of the world, *Have mercy on us!*
God the Holy Spirit, *Have mercy on us!*
Holy Trinity, one God, *Have mercy on us!*

Blood of Christ, only-begotten Son of the Eternal Father,
save us!
Blood of Christ, Incarnate Word of God, *save us!*
Blood of Christ, of the New and Eternal Testament, *save us!*
Blood of Christ, falling upon the earth in the Agony, *save us!*
Blood of Christ, shed profusely in the Scourging, *save us!*
Blood of Christ, flowing forth in the Crowning with Thorns,
save us!
Blood of Christ, poured out on the cross, *save us!*
Blood of Christ, price of our salvation, *save us!*
Blood of Christ, without which there is no forgiveness,
save us!

Blood of Christ, Eucharistic drink and refreshment of souls,
save us!

Blood of Christ, stream of mercy, *save us!*

Blood of Christ, victor over demons, *save us!*

Blood of Christ, courage of martyrs, *save us!*

Blood of Christ, strength of confessors, *save us!*

Blood of Christ, bringing forth virgins, *save us!*

Blood of Christ, help of those in peril, *save us!*

Blood of Christ, relief of the burdened, *save us!*

Blood of Christ, solace in sorrow, *save us!*

Blood of Christ, hope of the penitent, *save us!*

Blood of Christ, consolation of the dying, *save us!*

Blood of Christ, peace and tenderness of hearts, *save us!*

Blood of Christ, pledge of Eternal Life, *save us!*

Blood of Christ, freeing souls from Purgatory, *save us!*

Blood of Christ, most worthy of all glory and honor, *save us!*

Lamb of God, Who takes away the sins of the world, *Spare us, O Lord!*

Lamb of God, Who takes away the sins of the world, *Graciously hear us, O Lord!*

Lamb of God, Who takes away the sins of the world, *Have mercy on us!*

V. You have redeemed us, O Lord, in your blood.

R. And made us, for our God, a kingdom.

Let us pray.

Almighty and Eternal God, You have appointed your only begotten Son the
Redeemer of the world, and willed to be appeased by his Blood. Grant, we beg
of you, that we may worthily adore this price of our salvation, and through its
power be safeguarded from the evils of this present life, so that we may rejoice in
its fruits forever in heaven. Through the same Christ our Lord. Amen.

REFERENCES

Cover Image: *La Última Cena*, Juan de Juanes. Public Domain.

Preface quote: Blessed Dina Bélanger, *Autobiography* (Montreal, Canada: Les Religieuses de Jesus-Marie, 1997), 259.

January Image: *The Apparition of The Eucharist To San Pascual Bailon*, Vicente López Portaña (1772-1850). Public Domain.

January 1: Pope Benedict XVI, *God's Revolution, World Youth Day and Other Cologne Talks*, p. 23. Ignatius Press, 2006, San Francisco, CA.

January 2: St. Alphonsus Ligouri, *The Sermons of St. Alphonsus Liguori*, Fourth Edition, p. 235. TAN Books, 1982, Charlotte, NC.

January 3: St. Paul VI, *Mysterium Fidei*, n. 64.

January 4: St. Stanislaus Papczyński, *Saint Stanislaus Papczyński Selected Writings*, Trans. Casimir Krzyzanowski, MIC, Patrick Lynch, MIC, Thaddaeus Lancton, MIC, and J.R. Thomas Holland, p. 659-660. Marian Heritage, 2022, Stockbridge, MA.

January 5: St. John Vianney, as quoted in *Thoughts of the Cure D'Ars*, Compiled and Arranged by W. M. B., p. 22. TAN Books, 1984, Charlotte, NC.

January 6: *The Catechism of the Council of Trent*, Trans. John A. McHugh, O.P. and Charles J Callan, O.P., p. 246, TAN Books, 1982, Charlotte, NC.

January 7: St. Bonaventure, as quoted in St. Alphonsus Ligouri, *The Sermons of St. Alphonsus Liguori*, Fourth Edition, p. 237, TAN Books, 1982, Charlotte, NC.

January 8: *Catechism of the Catholic Church*, par. 1324.

January 9: St. Augustine of Hippo, as quoted in *The Catechism of the Council of Trent*, Trans. John A. McHugh, O.P. and Charles J Callan, O.P., p. 249. TAN Books, 1982, Charlotte, NC.

January 10: St. Irenaeus, from the treatise Against Heresies, *The Liturgy of the Hours, Vol. II*, p. 728. Catholic Book Publishing Corp, 1976, New York.

January 11: St. Cyril of Jerusalem as quoted in Pope St. Paul VI, *Mysterium Fidei*, n. 48.

January 12: St. Peter Julian Eymard, *How To Get More Out Of Holy Communion*, ch. 2 p. 11. Sophia Institute Press, 2000, Manchester, NH.

January 13: St. Hilary, as quoted in *The Catechism of the Council of Trent*, Trans. John A. McHugh, O.P. and Charles J Callan, O.P., p. 243, TAN Books, 1982, Charlotte, NC.

January 14: St. Claude De La Colombière, *The Spiritual Direction of Saint Claude De La Colombière,* Third Edition, Trans. Mother M. Philip, I.B.V.M., p. 29. Ignatius Press, 2018, San Francisco, CA.

January 15: St. Cyril of Alexandria, from a commentary on the gospel of John, *The Liturgy of the Hours, Vol. II*, p. 744. Catholic Book Publishing Corp, 1976, New York.

January 16: St. Lawrence Justinian, as quoted in St. Alphonsus Ligouri, *The Sermons of St. Alphonsus Liguori*, Fourth Edition, p. 236. TAN Books, 1982, Charlotte, NC.

January 17: Ven. Fulton J. Sheen, *Life of Christ*, p. 399. Image Books/Doubleday, 2008, New York.

January 18: St. Catherine of Siena, as quoted in Fr. Romanus Cessario, O.P., *Compassionate Blood, Catherine of Siena on the Passion*, p. 84. Magnificat, 2016, New York.

January 19: St. John Vianney, as quoted in *Thoughts of the Cure D'Ars*, Compiled and Arranged by W. M. B., p. 8. TAN Books, 1984, Charlotte, NC.

January 20: St. Francisco Marto, as quoted in *Blessed Francisco of Fatima*, Compiled by Msgr. Joseph A. Cirrincione, p. 37. TAN Books, 2016, Charlotte, NC.

January 21: St. Augustine of Hippo, as quoted in *The Catechism of the Council of Trent*, Trans. John A. McHugh, O.P. and Charles J Callan, O.P., p. 265. TAN Books, 1982, Charlotte, NC.

January 22: St. Faustina Kowalska, *Diary: Divine Mercy in My Soul*, 1811. Marian Press, 2005, Stockbridge, MA.

January 23: Thomas à Kempis, *The Imitation of Christ*. Trans. Ronald Knox, bk. 4, no. 4, 232. Ignatius Press, 2005, San Francisco.

January 24: St. Francis De Sales, *Introduction to the Devout Life*, ch. 21, 68. Ignatius Press, San Francisco, CA and Lighthouse Catholic Media, 2015, DeKalb, IL.

January 25: St. Paul, 1 Corinthians 10: 16-17, *Divine Mercy Catholic Bible, Revised Standard Version, Second Catholic Edition*, revised According to Liturgiam Authenticam, p. 1487-1488. Ascension Publishing, LCC, 2001, West Chester, PA.

January 26: Bl. Carlo Acutis, as quoted in *I Am With You, A Documentary on Carlo Acutis*, Eternal Word Television Network, 2021, Irondale, AL.

January 27: St. John Chrystostom as quoted in Pope St. Paul VI, *Mysterium Fidei*, n. 49.

January 28: St. Thomas Aquinas as quoted in *The Aquinas Prayer Book. The Prayers and Hymns of St. Thomas Aquinas*, trans. Robert Anderson and Johann Moser, p. 69. Sophia Institute Press, 2000, Manchester, NH.

January 29: St. Faustina Kowalska, *Diary: Divine Mercy in My Soul*, 476. Marian Press, 2005, Stockbridge, MA.

January 30: St. Francis Xavier Bianchi, as quoted in in Fr. Stefano M. Manelli, FI, *Jesus Our Eucharistic Love*, p. 21. Academy of the Immaculate, 2017, New Bedford, MA.

January 31: St. Hilary of Poitiers, as quoted in Pope Benedict XVI, "Message of His Holiness Benedict XVI for the Sixteenth World Day of the Sick," January 11, 2008, p. 2.

February Image: *The Holy Eucharist*, Artist Unknown.

February 1: St. Peter Julian Eymard, *How To Get More Out Of Holy Communion*, ch. 1, pg. 5. Sophia Institute Press, 2000, Manchester, NH.

February 2: Bl. James Alberione, as quoted in Fr. Stefano Manelli, FI, "Marian Coredemption in the Hagiography of the 20th Century," in *Mary at the Foot of the Cross: Acts from the International Symposium on Marian Coredemption*, p. 225. Academy of the Immaculate, 2001, New Bedford, MA.

February 3: Bl. Henry Suso, as quoted in Saint Joseph Adoration Monastery, *Manual for Eucharistic Adoration, The Poor Clares of Perpetual Adoration*, p. 118. TAN Books, 2016, Charlotte, NC.

February 4: St. John Vianney, as quoted in *Thoughts of the Cure D'Ars*, compiled and arranged by W. M. B., p. 29. TAN Books, 1984, Charlotte, NC.

February 5: Ven. Fulton J Sheen, *Calvary And The Mass*, p. 47. Coalition in Support of *Ecclesia Dei*, 1996, Glenview, IL.

February 6: St. Francis De Sales, *Introduction to the Devout Life*, ch. 21, p. 68. Lighthouse Catholic Media, 2015, San Francisco, CA.

February 7: St. Faustina Kowalska, *Diary: Divine Mercy in My Soul*, no. 1070. Marian Press, 2005 Stockbridge, MA.

February 8: Pope Leo XIII, *Mirae Caritatis (On the Holy Eucharist)*, 16.

February 9: St. Stanislaus Papczyński, as quoted in Andrzej Pakula, MIC, *Spirituality of the Religious Life according to Saint Stanislaus Papczyński and the Early Tradition of the Congregation of Marian Fathers*, p. 247-248. Marian Heritage, 2022, Stockbridge, MA.

February 10: St. Teresa of Calcutta, as quoted in Jose Luis Gonzalez Balado, *Mother Teresa In My Own Words*, p. 11. Liguori Publications, 1997, Liguori, MO.

February 11: Vatican Council II, *Lumen Gentium*, ch. 3

February 12: The Acts of the Apostles 2:42, *Divine Mercy Catholic Bible, Revised Standard Version, Second Catholic Edition*, revised according to Liturgiam Authenticam, p. 1425. Ascension Publishing, LCC, 2001, West Chester, PA.

February 13: St. Peter Julian Eymard, *Month of St. Joseph*, p. 51. Emmanuel Publications, 1948, Cleveland, OH.

February 14: St. Faustina Kowalska, *Diary: Divine Mercy in My Soul*, no. 1447. Marian Press, 2005, Stockbridge, MA.

February 15: St. Claude De La Colombière, *The Spiritual Direction of Saint Claude De La Colombière*, Third Edition, trans. Mother M. Philip, I.B.V.M.. p. 27. Ignatius Press, 2018, San Francisco, CA.

February 16: St. John Vianney, as quoted in *Thoughts of the Cure D'Ars*, compiled and arranged by W. M. B., p. 69. TAN Books, 1984, Charlotte, NC.

February 17: *Catechism of the Catholic Church*, 1325.

February 18: Ven. Fulton J. Sheen, *Life of Christ*, p. 402. Image Books/Doubleday, 2008, New York.

February 19: St. Padre Pio, as quoted in Gianluigi Pasquale, *Padre Pio's Spiritual Direction For Every Day*, trans. Marsha Daigle-Williamson, PH.D., p. 114. Servant, 2011, Cincinnati, OH.

February 20: St. Teresa of Ávila, *The Way of Perfection*, p. 217. TAN Books, 2010, Charlotte, NC.

February 21: Pope St. John Paul II, *Ecclesia de Eucharistia*, 31.

February 22: St. Catherine of Genoa, as quoted in Don Cattaneo Marabotto, *The Spiritual Doctrine of St. Catherine of Genoa*, p. 11. TAN Books and Publishers, Inc., 1989, Rockford, IL.

February 23: Thomas à Kempis, *The Imitation of Christ*, trans. Ronald Knox, bk. 4, no. 12, 249. Ignatius Press, 2005, San Francisco, CA.

February 24: Bl. William Joseph Chaminade, *Marian Writings: Volume 2*, p. 280. Marianist Resources Commission, 1980, Dayton, OH.

February 25: St. Thomas Aquinas, as quoted in Saint Joseph Adoration Monastery, *Manual for Eucharistic Adoration, The Poor Clares of Perpetual Adoration*, p. 108. TAN Books, 2016, Charlotte, NC.

February 26: St. John Bosco, as quoted in Fr. Stefano M. Manelli, FI, *Jesus Our Eucharistic Love*, p. 22-23. Academy of the Immaculate, 2017, New Bedford, MA.

February 27: St. John Vianney, as quoted in *Thoughts of the Cure D'Ars*, compiled and arranged by W. M. B., p. 65. TAN Books, 1984, Charlotte, NC.

February 28: St. Faustina Kowalska, *Diary: Divine Mercy in My Soul*, no. 914, Marian Press, 2005, Stockbridge, MA.

February 29: *Catechism of the Catholic Church*, 1340.

March Image: *The Glorification of the Eucharist*, Peter Paul Rubens (1577-1640). Public Domain.

March 1: St. Faustina Kowalska, *Diary: Divine Mercy in My Soul*, (no. 1385. Marian Press, 2005, Stockbridge, MA.

March 2: St. Peter Julian Eymard, *How To Get More Out Of Holy Communion*, ch. 2, p. 14. Sophia Institute Press, 2000, Manchester, NH.

March 3: St. Thérèse of Lisieux, *The Story of a Soul*, trans. John Beevers, ch. 5, p. 57. Image, 2001, New York.

March 4: Thomas à Kempis, *The Imitation of Christ*, trans. Ronald Knox, bk. 4, no. 4, 233. Ignatius Press, 2005, San Francisco, CA.

March 5: St. Isaac Jogues, as quoted in Francis Talbot, S.J., *Saint Among Savages, the Life of Saint Isaac Jogues*, p. 387. Ignatius Press, 2002, San Francisco, CA.

March 6: St. Catherine of Genoa, as quoted in Don Cattaneo Marabotto, *The Spiritual Doctrine of St. Catherine of Genoa*, p. 11. TAN Books and Publishers, Inc., 1989, Rockford, IL.

March 7: St. Cyril of Alexandria, from a commentary on the Gospel of John, *The Liturgy of the Hours, Vol. II*, p. 744. Catholic Book Publishing Corp, 1979, New York.

March 8: *Constitution on the Sacred Liturgy* (*Sacrosanctum Concilium*, 1963), Art. 47; S.C.R. Instruction *Eucharisticum Mysterium*, n. 3a, b.

March 9: Pope Benedict XVI, *God's Revolution, World Youth Day and Other Cologne Talks,* p. 57. Ignatius Press, 2006, San Francisco, CA.

March 10: Pope Leo XIII, *On The Holy Eucharist* (*Mirae Caritatis,* 1902), 19.

March 11: St. John Vianney, as quoted in *Thoughts of the Cure D'Ars*, compiled and arranged by W. M. B., p. 49. TAN Books, 1984, Charlotte, NC.

March 12: St. Francis De Sales, *Introduction to the Devout Life*, ch. 20, 65. Ignatius Press, San Francisco, CA and Lighthouse Catholic Media, 2015, DeKalb, IL.

March 13: St. Elizabeth Ann Seton, as quoted in Ellin Kelly and Annabelle Meliville, *Elizabeth Seton Selected Writings*, p. 168. Paulist Press, 1987, New York.

March 14: St. Faustina Kowalska, *Diary: Divine Mercy in My Soul*, no. 1392, Marian Press, 2005, Stockbridge, MA.

March 15: Ven. Fulton J. Sheen, *Life of Christ*, p. 402, Image Books/Doubleday, 2008, New York.

March 16: *Catechism of the Catholic Church*, 1326.

March 17: St. Claude De La Colombière, *The Spiritual Direction of Saint Claude De La Colombière*. Third Edition, trans. Mother M. Philip, I.B.V.M., p. 30, Ignatius Press, 2018, San Francisco, CA.

March 18: St. Cyril of Jerusalem as quoted in Pope St. Paul VI, *Mysterium Fidei*, n. 30.

March 19: Pope St. John Paul II, *Homily at the Shrine of St. Joseph in Kalisz, Poland*, June 4, 1997.

March 20: St. Elizabeth Ann Seton, as quoted in Ellin Kelly and Annabelle Meliville, *Elizabeth Seton Selected Writings*, p. 167. Paulist Press, 1987, New York.

March 21: Bl. Pope Pius IX, *Quemadmodum Deus* (December 8, 1870).

March 22: St. Joseph Marello, as quoted in Larry Toschi, OSJ, *St. Joseph in the Lives of Two Blesseds of the Church: Blessed Junipero Serra and Blessed Joseph Marello*, p. 78, Guardian of the Redeemer Books, 1994, Santa Cruz, CA.

March 23: St. Teresa of Calcutta, as quoted in Jose Luis Gonzalez Balado, *Mother Teresa In My Own Words*, p. 97. Liguori Publications, 1997, Liguori, MO.

March 24: St. Alphonsus Ligouri, *The Sermons of St. Alphonsus Liguori*, Fourth Edition, p. 235. TAN Books, 1982, Charlotte, NC.

March 25: Pope St. John Paul II, *The Church from the Eucharist (Ecclesia de Eucharistia,* 2003), 55.

March 26: Venerable Fulton J. Sheen, *The World's First Love: Mary, Mother of God*, p. 37. Ignatius Press, 1952, San Francisco, CA.

March 27: St. Charles de Foucauld, as quoted in Dennis J. Billy, C.Ss.R., *The Mystery of the Eucharist, Voices from the Saints and Mystics*, p. 274. New City Press, 2014, Hyde Park, NY.

March 28: St. Teresa of Ávila, *The Way of Perfection*, p. 204. TAN Books, 2010, Charlotte, NC.

March 29: St. Thérèse of Lisieux, *The Story of a Soul*, trans. John Beevers, ch. 5, 57. Image, 2001, New York.

March 30: St. John Vianney, as quoted in *Thoughts of the Cure D'Ars*, compiled and arranged by W. M. B., p. 45. TAN Books, 1984, Charlotte, NC.

March 31: St. Peter Julian Eymard, *Month of St. Joseph*, p. 32. Emmanuel Publications, 1948, Cleveland, OH.

April Image: *The Last Supper*, Pierre Landry (1630?–1701). Public Domain

April 1: St. Teresa of Ávila, *The Way of Perfection*, p. 209. TAN Books, 2010, Charlotte, NC.

April 2: St. Ignatius of Loyola, as quoted in Fr. Lukas Etlin, O.S.B. *The Holy Eucharist, Our All*, p. 2. TAN Books, 1999, Charlotte, NC.

April 3: Vatican Council II *Lumen Gentium*, ch. 7

April 4: St. Faustina Kowalska, *Diary: Divine Mercy in My Soul*, no. 1826, Marian Press, 2005, Stockbridge, MA.

April 5: St. Padre Pio, as quoted in Gianluigi Pasquale, *Padre Pio's Spiritual Direction For Every Day*, trans. Marsha Daigle-Williamson, PH.D., p. 84. Servant, 2011, Cincinnati, OH.

April 6: St. Peter Julian Eymard, *How To Get More Out Of Holy Communion*, ch. 5, 35, Sophia Institute Press, 2000, Manchester, NH.

April 7: St. Hilary, from the treatise On the Trinity, *The Liturgy of the Hours, Vol. III*, p. 779. Catholic Book Publishing Corp, 1976, New York.

April 8: St. Faustina Kowalska, *Diary: Divine Mercy in My Soul*, no. 1509. Marian Press, 2005, Stockbridge, MA.

April 9: St. John Vianney, as quoted in *Thoughts of the Cure D'Ars*, compiled and arranged by W. M. B., p. 52. TAN Books, 1984, Charlotte, NC.

April 10: *The Catechism of the Council of Trent*, trans. John A. McHugh, O.P. and Charles J Callan, O.P., p. 227. TAN Books, 1982, Charlotte, NC.

April 11: St. Gemma Galgani, as quoted in Bob Lord and Penny Lord, *Visionaries, Mystics and Stigmatists Down Through the Ages*, p. 324. Journeys of Faith, 1995.

April 12: St. Ignatius of Loyola, as quoted in Fr. Lukas Etlin, O.S.B., *The Holy Eucharist, Our All*, p. 2. TAN Books, 1999, Charlotte, NC.

April 13: St. Pius X, as quoted in Fr. Lukas Etlin, O.S.B. *The Holy Eucharist, Our All*, p. 33. TAN Books, 1999, Charlotte, NC.

April 14: Ven. Fulton J. Sheen, *Life of Christ*, p. 403. Image Books/Doubleday, 2008, New York.

April 15: St. John Vianney, as quoted in George W. Rutler, *Cure D'Ars Saint John Vianney*, p. 11. The Incorporated Catholic Truth Society of London, 2009, San Francisco, CA.

April 16: St. Bernadette Soubirous, as quoted in Fr. Stefano M. Manelli, FI, *Jesus Our Eucharistic Love*, p. 113. Academy of the Immaculate, 2017, New Bedford, MA.

April 17: St. Luke: 24: 30-35, *Divine Mercy Catholic Bible, Revised Standard Version, Second Catholic Edition*, revised according to Liturgiam Authenticam, p. 1386. Ascension Publishing LLC, 2001, West Chester, PA.

April 18: St. Catherine of Genoa, as quoted in Fr. Stefano M. Manelli, FI, *Jesus Our Eucharistic Love*, p. 58. Academy of the Immaculate, 2017, New Bedford, MA.

April 19: Pope St. John Paul II, *Ecclesia de Eucharistia*, 56.

April 20: Thomas à Kempis, *The Imitation of Christ*, trans. Ronald Knox, bk. 4, no. 13, 250, Ignatius Press, 2005, San Francisco, CA.

April 21: St. Anselm of Canterbury, as quoted in Dennis J. Billy, C.Ss.R., *The Mystery of the Eucharist, Voices from the Saints and Mystics*, p. 43. New City Press, 2014, Hyde Park, NY.

April 22: St. Teresa of Calcutta, as quoted in Jose Luis Gonzalez Balado, *Mother Teresa In My Own Words*, p. 97, Liguori Publications, 1997, Liguori, MO.

April 23: Bl. Concepción Cabrera de Armida, *Roses and Thorns*, p. 82. Society of St. Paul, 2007, Staten Island, NY.

April 24: Pope Leo XIII, *Mirae Caritatis (On the Holy Eucharist)*, 7.

April 25: St. Mark 14: 22-25, *Divine Mercy Catholic Bible, Revised Standard Version, Second Catholic Edition*, revised according to Liturgiam Authenticam, p. 1334. Ascension Publishing, LLC, 2001, West Chester, PA.

April 26: St. Faustina Kowalska, *Diary: Divine Mercy in My Soul*, no. 1826. Marian Press, 2005, Stockbridge, MA.

April 27: St. John Vianney, as quoted in *Thoughts of the Cure D'Ars*, compiled and arranged by W. M. B., p. 74. TAN Books, 1984, Charlotte, NC.

April 28: St. Louis de Montfort, *True Devotion to Mary*, p. 170-171. TAN Books, 1985, Rockford, IL.

April 29: St. Catherine of Siena, as quoted in Fr. Romanus Cessario, O.P., *Compassionate Blood, Catherine of Siena on the Passion*, p. 85. Magnificat, 2016, New York.

April 30: St. John Damascene, as quoted in Dennis J. Billy, C.Ss.R., *The Mystery of the Eucharist, Voices from the Saints and Mystics*, p. 31. New City Press, 2014, Hyde Park.

May Image: *Triumph of the Eucharist* (detail), Peter Paul Rubens (1577-1640). Adobe Stock.

May 1: Ven. Fulton J. Sheen, *The World's First Love: Mary, Mother of God*, p. 245. Ignatius Press, 1996, San Francisco, CA.

May 2: St. Teresa of Ávila, *The Way of Perfection*, p. 212. TAN Books, 2010, Charlotte, NC.

May 3: St. Francis De Sales, *Introduction to the Devout Life*, ch. 14, 55, Ignatius Press, San Francisco, CA and Lighthouse Catholic Media, 2015, DeKalb, IL.

May 4: St. Alphonsus Ligouri, *The Sermons of St. Alphonsus Liguori*, fourth edition, p. 235. TAN Books, 1982, Charlotte, NC.

May 5: Pope St. John Paul II, *Ecclesia de Eucharistia*, 37.

May 6: St. Ignatius of Loyola, *The Spiritual Exercises of Saint Ignatius or Manresa*, p. 204. TAN Books, 2010, Charlotte, NC.

May 7: *Catechism of the Catholic Church*, 1328.

May 8: St. Mary Magdalene de'Pazzi, as quoted in Fr. Stefano M. Manelli, FI, *Jesus Our Eucharistic Love*, p. 45. Academy of the Immaculate, 2017, New Bedford, MA.

May 9: Pope Leo XIII, *Mirae Caritatis (On the Holy Eucharist)*, 9.

May 10: St. Peter Damian, *Sermo XLV In Nativitate Beatissimae Virginis Mariae*: pl 144, 740-748.

May 11: St. John Vianney, as quoted in *Thoughts of the Cure D'Ars*, compiled and arranged by W. M. B., p. 72. TAN Books, 1984, Charlotte, NC.

May 12: St. Anthony of Padua, as quoted in Luigi Gambero, SM, *Mary in the Middle Ages: The Blessed Virgin Mary in the Thought of Medieval Latin Theologians*, trans. Thomas Buffer, p. 204. Ignatius Press, San Francisco CA.

May 13: St. Philip Neri, as quoted in Fr. Stefano M. Manelli, FI, *Jesus Our Eucharistic Love,* p. 59. Academy of the Immaculate, 2017, New Bedford, MA.

May 14: St. Francis De Sales, *Introduction to the Devout Life,* ch. 20, 65. Ignatius Press, San Francisco, CA: and Lighthouse Catholic Media, 2015, DeKalb, IL.

May 15: St. Charles De Foucauld, as quoted in Jean-Jacques Antier, *Charles De Foucauld (Charles Of Jesus),* p. 154. Ignatius Press, 2022, San Francisco, CA.

May 16: St. Faustina Kowalska, *Diary: Divine Mercy in My Soul,* no. 1407, Marian Press, 2005, Stockbridge, MA.

May 17: St. Paschal Baylon, as quoted in Saint Joseph Adoration Monastery, *Manual for Eucharistic Adoration, The Poor Clares of Perpetual Adoration,* p. 106. TAN Books, 2016, Charlotte, NC.

May 18: St. Stanislaus Papczyński, *Saint Stanislaus Papczyński Selected Writings,* trans. Casimir Krzyzanowski, MIC, Patrick Lynch, MIC, Thaddaeus Lancton, MIC, and J.R. Thomas Holland, p. 659. Marian Heritage, 2022, Stockbridge, MA.

May 19: Thomas à Kempis, *The Imitation of Chris,* trans. Ronald Knox, Bk 4, no. 14, p. 251-252. Ignatius Press, 2005, San Francisco, CA.

May 20: Blessed Basil Moreau, *Basil Moreau: Essential Writings,* edited by Kevin Grove, CSC and Andrew Gawrych, CSC, p. 165. Christian Classics, 2014, Notre Dame, IN.

May 21: St. Anthony Mary Claret, as quoted in Fr. Juan Echevarria, CMF, *The Miracles of Saint Anthony Mary Claret,* p. 240. TAN Books, 1992, Rockford, IL.

May 22: St. Thomas Aquinas, as quoted in Francois Mauriac, *Holy Thursday, The Night That Changed The World,* p. 88. Sophia Institute Press, 1991, Manchester, NH.

May 23: St. Gregory VII as quoted in Pope St. Paul VI, *Mysterium Fidei,* n. 52.

May 24: Blessed Basil Moreau, *Basil Moreau: Essential Writings.* Edited by Kevin Grove, CSC and Andrew Gawrych, CSC, p. 129-130. Christian Classics, 2014, Notre Dame, IN.

May 25: St. Mary Magdalene de'Pazzi, as quoted in Fr. Stefano M. Manelli, FI, *Jesus Our Eucharistic Love,* p. 42. Academy of the Immaculate, 2017, New Bedford, MA.

May 26: St. Philip Neri, as quoted in Fr. Stefano M. Manelli, FI, *Jesus Our Eucharistic Love,* p. 59. Academy of the Immaculate, 2017, New Bedford, MA.

May 27: St. Teresa of Calcutta, as quoted in Jose Luis Gonzalez Balado, *Mother Teresa In My Own Words,* p. 105. Liguori Publications, 1997, Liguori, MO.

May 28: St. Leo the Great, from a sermon by St. Leo the Great, pope. *The Liturgy of the Hours Vol. II,* p. 661. Catholic Book Publishing Corp, 1976, New York.

May 29: St. Catherine of Siena, as quoted in Dennis J. Billy, C.Ss.R., *The Mystery of the Eucharist, Voices from the Saints and Mystics,* p. 144-145. New City Press, 2014, Hyde Park, NY.

May 30: St. Joan of Arc, as quoted in Mark Twain, *Joan of Arc,* trans. Jean Francois Alden, p. 386. Ignatius Press, 2007, San Francisco, CA.

May 31: Pope St. John Paul II, *Ecclesia de Eucharistia,* 55.

June Image: *The symbolic fresco Jesus give the communion in church Pfarrkirche Kaisermühlen.* Adobe Stock.

June 1: St. Justin, Martyr, from the First Apology in Defense of the Christians, *The Liturgy of the Hours Vol II,* p. 694 Catholic Books Publishing Corp, 1976, New York.

June 2: Bl. Crescentia of Kaufbeuren, as quoted in Fr. Lukas Etlin, O.S.B., *The Holy Eucharist, Our All,* p. 61. TAN Books, 1999, Charlotte, NC.

June 3: St. Teresa of Calcutta, as quoted in Francois Mauriac, *Holy Thursday, The Night That Changed The World,* p. ii. Sophia Institute Press, 1991, Manchester, NH.

June 4: Blessed Basil Moreau, *Basil Moreau: Essential Writings,* edited by Kevin Grove, CSC and Andrew Gawrych, CSC, p. 166. Christian Classics, 2014, Notre Dame, IN.

June 5: Servant of God Frank Duff, *Legio Mariae: The Official Handbook of the Legion of Mary,* p. 139. De Montfort House, 1975, Dublin, Ireland.

June 6: St. Francis De Sales, *Introduction to the Devout Life,* ch. 20, 65. Ignatius Press San Francisco, CA and Lighthouse Catholic Media, 2015, DeKalb, IL.

June 7: Pope St. Paul VI, *Mysterium Fidei,* n. 67.

June 8: St. John Vianney, as quoted in *Thoughts of the Cure D'Ars,* compiled and arranged by W. M. B. p. 57. TAN Books, 1984, Charlotte, NC.

June 9: Ven. Andrew Beltrami, as quoted in Fr. Stefano M. Manelli, FI, *Jesus Our Eucharistic Love,* p. 64. Academy of the Immaculate, 2017, New Bedford, MA.

June 10: St. Anthony Mary Claret, as quoted in Fr. Juan Echevarria, CMF, *The Miracles of Saint Anthony Mary Claret,* p. 239. TAN Books, 1992, Rockford, IL.

June 11: St. Peter Julian Eymard, *How To Get More Out Of Holy Communion,* ch. 3, 19. Sophia Institute Press, 2000, Manchester, NH.

June 12: St. Teresa of Ávila, *The Way of Perfection*, p. 209, TAN Books, 2010, Charlotte, NC.

June 13: St. Gemma Galgani, as quoted in Bob Lord and Penny Lord, *Visionaries, Mystics and Stigmatists Down Through the Ages*, p. 324. Journeys of Faith, 1995.

June 14: Bl. Concepción Cabrera de Armida, *Roses and Thorns*, p. 82. Society of St. Paul, 2007, Staten Island, NY.

June 15: St. Faustina Kowalska, *Diary: Divine Mercy in My Soul*, no. 1721. Marian Press, 2005, Stockbridge, MA.

June 16: St. Alphonsus Ligouri, *The Sermons of St. Alphonsus Liguori*, fourth edition, p. 235. TAN Books, 1982, Charlotte, NC.

June 17: Thomas à Kempis, *The Imitation of Christ,* trans. Ronald Knox, bk. 4, no. 16, 255. Ignatius Press, 2005, San Francisco, CA.

June 18: St. John Damascene, as quoted in Dennis J. Billy, C.Ss.R., *The Mystery of the Eucharist, Voices from the Saints and Mystics*, p. 35. New City Press, 2014, Hyde Park, NY.

June 19: Pope Urban IV, as quoted in Timothy P. O'Malley, *Real Presence. What Does It Mean and Why Does It Matter?* p. 16. Ave Maria Press, 2021, Notre Dame, IN.

June 20: St. Padre Pio, as quoted in Gianluigi Pasquale, *Padre Pio's Spiritual Direction For Every Day*, trans. Marsha Daigle-Williamson, PH.D., p. 190. Servant, 2011, Cincinnati, OH.

June 21: St. Teresa of Ávila, *The Way of Perfection*, p. 203. TAN Books, 2010, Charlotte, NC.

June 22: Pope St. John Paul II, *Ecclesia de Eucharistia*, 25.

June 23: St. Josemaria Escrivá, *Christ is Passing By,* p. 345. Scepter, 1973, New York, NY.

June 24: Bl. William Joseph Chaminade, *Marian Writings: Volume 1*, p. 173. Marianist Resources Commission, 1980, Dayton, OH.

June 25: St. Gertrude, as quoted in Servant of God Fr. Lukas Etlin, O.S.B., *Devotion To The Sacred Heart*, p. 11, TAN Books, 2012, Charlotte, NC.

June 26: St. John Vianney, as quoted in *Thoughts of the Cure D'Ars*, compiled and arranged by W. M. B., p. 15. TAN Books, 1984, Charlotte, NC.

June 27: St. Cyril of Alexandria as quoted in Pope St. Paul VI, *Mysterium Fidei*, n. 60.

June 28: St. Irenaeus, from the treatise Against Heresies, *The Liturgy of the Hours Vol. II*, p. 727. Catholic Books Publishing Corp, 1976, New York.

June 29: 1 Peter 1:18-20, *Divine Mercy Catholic Bible, Revised Standard Version, Second Catholic Edition*, revised according To Liturgiam Authenticam, p. 1567. Ascension Publishing, LLC, 2001, West Chester, PA.

June 30: St. Alphonsus de Liguori, *The Complete Works of Saint Alphonsus De Liguori, The Ascetical Works, Vol. VI., The Centenary Edition, The Holy Eucharist*, p. 190. Benziger Brothers, 1887, New York.

July Image: *Stained Glass - Priest giving Holy Communion* Adobe Stock.

July 1: St. Francis De Sales, *Introduction to the Devout Life*, ch. 21, 68. Ignatius Press, San Francisco, CA and Lighthouse Catholic Media, 2015, DeKalb, IL.

July 2: St. Charles de Foucauld, as quoted in Dennis J. Billy, C.Ss.R., *The Mystery of the Eucharist, Voices from the Saints and Mystics*, p. 275. New City Press, 2014, Hyde Park, NY.

July 3: Blessed James Alberione, *Mary, Mother and Model: Feasts of Mary*, p. 119. Daughters of St. Paul, 1958, Boston, MA.

July 4: Ven. Fulton J. Sheen, *Life of Christ*, p. 396. Image Books/Doubleday, 2008, New York.

July 5: St. Hilary, from the treatise On the Trinity, *The Liturgy of the Hours Vol. II*, p. 779-780. Catholic Books Publishing Corp, 1976, New York.

July 6: St. Maria Goretti, as quoted in Glynn MacNiven-Johnston, *Maria Goretti Teenage Martyr*, p. 14. Catholic Truth Society, 1997, London.

July 7: St. John Vianney, as quoted in *Thoughts of the Cure D'Ars*, compiled and arranged by W. M. B., p. 53. TAN Books, 1984, Charlotte, NC.

July 8: Angel of Peace, the Guardian Angel of Portugal, as quoted in *Our Lady of Fatima's Peace Plan From Heaven*, p. 2. TAN Books and Publishers, Inc., 1983, Rockford, IL.

July 9: St. Padre Pio, as quoted in Gianluigi Pasquale, *Padre Pio's Spiritual Direction For Every Day*, trans. Marsha Daigle-Williamson, PH.D., p. 192. Servant, 2011, Cincinnati, OH.

July 10: Pope St. John Paul II, *Ecclesia de Eucharistia*, 57.

July 11: St. Augustine, as quoted in Christopher Cardinal Schonborn, *The Source of Life, Exploring the Mystery of the Eucharist*, p. 102-103. Ignatius Press, 2013, San Francisco, CA.

July 12: Blessed Basil Moreau, *Basil Moreau: Essential Writings,* edited by Kevin Grove, CSC and Andrew Gawrych, CSC, p. 324. Christian Classics, 2014, Notre Dame, IN.

July 13: St. Damien of Molokai, as quoted in Fr. Florian Racine, *Could You Not Watch With Me One Hour?* p. 55. Ignatius Press, 2104, San Francisco, CA.

July 14: St. Teresa of Ávila, *The Way of Perfection*, p. 204-205. TAN Books, 2010, Charlotte, NC.

July 15: St. Bonaventure as quoted in Pope St. Paul VI, *Mysterium Fidei*, n. 20.

July 16: Pope St. John Paul II, *Ecclesia de Eucharistia*, 57.

July 17: *The Catechism of the Council of Trent*, trans. John A. McHugh, O.P. and Charles J Callan, O.P., p. 249. TAN Books, 1982, Charlotte, NC.

July 18: St. Thomas Aquinas, as quoted in Francois Mauriac, *Holy Thursday, The Night That Changed The World*, p. 77, Sophia Institute Press, 1991, Manchester, NH.

July 19: Blessed Basil Moreau, *Basil Moreau: Essential Writings,* edited by Kevin Grove, CSC and Andrew Gawrych, CSC, p. 323. Christian Classics, 2014, Notre Dame, IN.

July 20: St. Teresa of Calcutta, as quoted in Francois Mauriac, *Holy Thursday, The Night That Changed The World*, p. ii. Sophia Institute Press, 1991, Manchester, NH.

July 21: St. Lawrence Brindisi, as quoted in Fr. Stefano M. Manelli, FI, *Jesus Our Eucharistic Love*, p. 22. Academy of the Immaculate, 2017, New Bedford, MA.

July 22: St. Peter Julian Eymard, *How To Get More Out Of Holy Communion*, ch 3, 20. Sophia Institute Press, 2000, Manchester, NH.

July 23: St. Stanislaus Papczyński, as quoted in Andrzej Pakula, MIC, *Spirituality of the Religious Life according to Saint Stanislaus Papczyński and the Early Tradition of the Congregation of Marian Fathers*, p. 249-250. Marian Heritage, 2022, Stockbridge, MA.

July 24: Servant of God Frank Duff, *Legio Mariae: The Official Handbook of the Legion of Mary*, p. 138. De Montfort House, 1975, Dublin, Ireland.

July 25: *Catechism of the Catholic Church*, par. 1335.

July 26: Ven. Fulton J. Sheen, *These Are The Sacraments*, p. 82. Image Books/ Doubleday, 1964, Garden City, NY.

July 27: St. Alphonsus Ligouri, *The Sermons of St. Alphonsus Liguori*, fourth edition, p. 236. TAN Books, 1982, Charlotte, NC.

July 28: St. John Vianney, as quoted in *Thoughts of the Cure D'Ars*, compiled and arranged by W. M. B., p. 47, TAN Books, 1984, Charlotte, NC.

July 29: Pope Leo XIII, *Mirae Caritatis On The Holy Eucharist*, 11.

July 30: Blessed James Alberione, *Mary, Mother and Model: Feasts of Mary*, p. 119. Daughters of St. Paul, 1958, Boston, MA.

July 31: St. Ignatius of Loyola as quoted in Pope St. Paul VI, *Mysterium Fidei*, n. 44.

August Image: *Faith and religion. Catholic church*. Adobe Stock.

August 1: St. Alphonsus Ligouri, *The Sermons of St. Alphonsus Liguori*, fourth edition, p. 233. TAN Books, 1982, Charlotte, NC.

August 2: St. Peter Julian Eymard, *How To Get More Out Of Holy Communion*, ch. 8, 58-59. Sophia Institute Press, 2000, Manchester, NH.

August 3: St. Gertrude the Great, as quoted in Saint Joseph Adoration Monastery, *Manual for Eucharistic Adoration, The Poor Clares of Perpetual Adoration*, p. 113. TAN Books, 2016, Charlotte, NC.

August 4: St. John Vianney, as quoted in *Thoughts of the Cure D'Ars*, compiled and arranged by W. M. B., p. 38. TAN Books, 1984, Charlotte, NC.

August 5: Blessed Basil Moreau, *Basil Moreau: Essential Writings,* edited by Kevin Grove, CSC and Andrew Gawrych, CSC, p. 130. Christian Classics, 2014, Notre Dame, IN.

August 6: St. John 6: 30-35, *Divine Mercy Catholic Bible, Revised Standard Version, Second Catholic Edition*, revised according to Liturgiam Authenticam p. 1397. Ascension Publishing LLC, 2001, West Chester, PA.

August 7: St. Thomas Aquinas, as quoted in Pope Leo XIII, *Mirae Caritatis (On The Holy Eucharist)*, 11.

August 8: St. Padre Pio, as quoted in Gianluigi Pasquale, *Padre Pio's Spiritual Direction For Every Day,* trans. Marsha Daigle-Williamson, PH.D., p. 258, Servant, 2011, Cincinnati, OH.

August 9: St. Charles de Foucauld, as quoted in Dennis J. Billy, C.Ss.R., *The Mystery of the Eucharist, Voices from the Saints and Mystics*, p. 269. New City Press, 2014, Hyde Park, NY.

August 10: St. Damien of Molokai, as quoted in Fr. Florian Racine, *Could You Not Watch With Me One Hour?* p. 55, Ignatius Press, 2014, San Francisco, CA.

August 11: St. Teresa of Calcutta, as quoted in Dennis J. Billy, C.Ss.R., *The Mystery of the Eucharist, Voices from the Saints and Mystics*, p. 298. New City Press, 2014, Hyde Park, NY.

August 12: Servant of God Frank Duff, *Legio Mariae: The Official Handbook of the Legion of Mary*, p. 137-138. De Montfort House, 1975, Dublin, Ireland.

August 13: St. Hippolytus as quoted in Pope St. Paul VI, *Mysterium Fidei*, n. 57.

August 14: St. Francis de Sales, as quoted in Rosalie Marie Levy, *Joseph the Just Man* (1955), 142.

August 15: St. Louis de Montfort, *True Devotion to Mary*, trans. Fr. William Faber, D.D., no. 196. TAN Books, 2010, Charlotte, NC.

August 16: Servant of God Luis Martinez, *Only Jesus*, trans. Sr. Mary St. Daniel, BVM., p. 120. Herder, 1962, St. Louis, MO.

August 17: Bl. Anne Catherine Emmerich, *The Dolorous Passion of Our Lord Jesus Christ*, meditation 8, 85. Burnes & Oates, 1928, London.

August 18: Bl. Basil Moreau, *Basil Moreau: Essential Writings*, edited by Kevin Grove, CSC and Andrew Gawrych, CSC, p. 128. Christian Classics, 2014, Notre Dame, IN.

August 19: St. Anthony Mary Claret, *Autobiography*, p. 241. Claretain Publications, 1976, Chicago, IL.

August 20: Bl. James Alberione, *Mary, Mother and Model: Feasts of Mary*, p. 120, Daughters of St. Paul, 1958, Boston, MA.

August 21: St. Pius X, as quoted in Fr. Stefano M. Manelli, FI, *Jesus Our Eucharistic Love*, p. ix. Academy of the Immaculate, 2017, New Bedford, MA.

August 22: St. Faustina Kowalska, *Diary: Divine Mercy in My Soul*, no. 1114. Marian Press, 2005, Stockbridge, MA.

August 23: St. Teresa of Ávila, *The Way of Perfection*, p. 211, TAN Books, 2010, Charlotte, NC.

August 24: Bl. Alexandrina da Costa, as quoted in *The Eucharistic Miracles of the World*, p. 266. Eternal Life, 2009, Bardstown, KY.

August 25: St. Louis IX, King of France, as quoted in in Fr. Stefano M. Manelli, FI, *Jesus Our Eucharistic Love*, p. 24. Academy of the Immaculate, 2017, New Bedford, MA.

August 26: St. Claude De La Colombière, *The Spiritual Direction of Saint Claude De La Colombière*, third edition, trans. Mother M. Philip, I.B.V.M., p. 29. Ignatius Press, 2018, San Francisco, CA.

August 27: St. Monica, as quoted in *The Confessions of Saint Augustine*, trans. John K. Ryan, p. 186. Image, 2014, New York.

August 28: St. Augustine of Hippo, as quoted in Pope St. Paul VI, *Mysterium Fidei*, n. 55.

August 29: St. Alphonsus Liguori, *Dignity and Duties of the Priest*, p. 227. Redemptorist Fathers, 1927, Brooklyn, NY.

August 30: St. Gaudentius of Brescia, from a sermon by St. Gaudentius of Brescia, bishop. *The Liturgy of the Hours Vol II*, p. 669. Catholic Book Publishing Corp, 1976, New York.

August 31: Ven. Praxedes Fernandez, as quoted in Fr. Martin-Maria Olive, OP, *Praxedes: Wife, Mother, Widow and Lay Dominican*, p. 77. TAN Books, 1987, Rockford, IL.

September Image: *The Triumph of the Church*, follower of Peter Paul Rubens. Public Domain.

September 1: St. Peter Julian Eymard, as quoted in Fr. Florian Racine, *Could You Not Watch With Me One Hour?* p. 171. Ignatius Press, 2014, San Francisco, CA.

September 2: St. John Damascene, as quoted in Dennis J. Billy, C.Ss.R., *The Mystery of the Eucharist, Voices from the Saints and Mystics*, p. 37-38. New City Press, 2014, Hyde Park, NY.

September 3: Ven. Fulton J. Sheen, *Life of Christ*, p. 398-399. Image Books/Doubleday, 2008, New York.

September 4: Blessed Dina Belanger, *Autobiography*, p. 259. Les Religieuses de Jesus-Marie, 1997, Montreal, Canada.

September 5: St. Teresa of Calcutta, as quoted in Francois Mauriac, *Holy Thursday, The Night That Changed The World*, p. ii. Sophia Institute Press, 1991, Manchester, NH.

September 6: Pope St. Paul VI, *Mysterium Fidei*, n. 67.

September 7: Servant of God Frank Duff, *Legio Mariae: The Official Handbook of the Legion of Mary*, p. 138. De Montfort House, 1975, Dublin, Ireland.

September 8: St. Peter Julian Eymard, *Our Lady of the Blessed Sacrament: Readings for the Month of May*, p. 31. Emmanuel Publications, 1930, Cleveland, Ohio.

September 9: St. Josemaria Escrivá, *Christ is Passing By*, p. 346. Scepter, 1973, New York, NY.

September 10: St. John Vianney, as quoted in *Thoughts of the Cure D'Ars*, compiled and arranged by W. M. B., p. 40. TAN Books, 1984, Charlotte, NC.

September 11: St. Peter Julian Eymard, *How To Get More Out Of Holy Communion*, ch. 3, 22. Sophia Institute Press, 2000, Manchester, NH.

September 12: Ven. Mary of Agreda, *The Mystical City of God. Vol. III*, trans. Rev. George J. Blatter, no. 484. TAN Books, 2006, Charlotte, NC.

September 13: Bl. Basil Moreau, *Basil Moreau: Essential Writings,* edited by Kevin Grove, CSC and Andrew Gawrych, CSC, p. 325. Christian Classics, 2014, Notre Dame, IN.

September 14: St. John Chrysostom as quoted in Pope St. Paul VI, *Mysterium Fidei*, n. 17.

September 15: St. Catherine of Genoa, as quoted in Don Cattaneo Marabotto, *The Spiritual Doctrine of St. Catherine of Genoa*, p. 12. TAN Books and Publishers, Inc., 1989, Rockford, IL.

September 16: St. Cyprian as quoted in Pope St. Paul VI, *Mysterium Fidei*, n. 42.

September 17: St. Josemaria Escrivá, *Christ is Passing By*, p. 347. Scepter, 1973, New York, NY.

September 18: St. Anthony Mary Claret, *Autobiography*, p. 139. Claretian, 1976, Chicago, IL.

September 19: Pope Leo XIII, *Mirae Caritatis On The Holy Eucharist*, 13.

September 20: St. Charles de Foucauld, as quoted in Dennis J. Billy, C.Ss.R., *The Mystery of the Eucharist, Voices from the Saints and Mystics*, p. 275. New City Press, 2014, Hyde Park, NY.

September 21: Bl. Basil Moreau, *Basil Moreau: Essential Writing,*. edited by Kevin Grove, CSC and Andrew Gawrych, CSC, p. 129. Christian Classics, 2014, Notre Dame, IN.

September 22: Pope St. John Paul II, *Redemptoris Mater,* 44.

September 23: St. Peter Damian, *Sermon XLV In Nativitate Beatissimae Virginis Mariae*: PL 144, 743C.

September 24: St. Teresa of Ávila, *The Way of Perfection*, p. 206. TAN Books, 2010, Charlotte, NC.

September 25: St. John Vianney, as quoted in George W. Rutler, *Cure D'Ars Saint John Vianney*, p. 11. The Incorporated Catholic Truth Society of London, 2009, San Francisco, CA.

September 26: Pope St. Paul VI, *Mysterium Fidei*, n. 34.

September 27: St. Vincent de Paul, as quoted in Fr. Stefano M. Manelli, FI, *Jesus Our Eucharistic Love*, p. 50. Academy of the Immaculate, 2017, New Bedford, MA.

September 28: St. Damien of Molokai, as quoted in Fr. Florian Racine, *Could You Not Watch With Me One Hour?* p.55, Ignatius Press, 2014, San Francisco, CA.

September 29: St. Padre Pio, as quoted in Fr. Florian Racine, *Could You Not Watch With Me One Hour?* p. 69. Ignatius Press, 2014, San Francisco, CA.

September 30: St. Claude De La Colombière, as quoted in Fr. Florian Racine, *Could You Not Watch With Me One Hour?* p. 211. Ignatius Press, 2014, San Francisco, CA.

October Image: *Last Communion of St. Lucy*, Giovanni Battista Tiepolo (1696–1770). Public Domain.

October 1: St. Peter Damian, *Sermon XLV In Nativitate Beatissimae Virginis Mariae*: PL 144, 743B.

October 2: St. John Chrysostom, as quoted in St. Alphonsus Ligouri, *The Sermons of St. Alphonsus Liguori*, fourth edition, p. 237. TAN Books, 1982, Charlotte, NC.

October 3: Ven. Fulton J. Sheen, as quoted in Saint Joseph Adoration Monastery, *Manual for Eucharistic Adoration, The Poor Clares of Perpetual Adoration*, p. 120. TAN Books, 2016, Charlotte, NC.

October 4: Pope Benedict XVI, as quoted in Fr. Florian Racine, *Could You Not Watch With Me One Hour?* p. 71. Ignatius Press, 2014, San Francisco, CA.

October 5: St. Faustina Kowalska, *Diary: Divine Mercy in My Soul*, no. 1804. Marian Press, 2005, Stockbridge, MA.

October 6: Ven. Fulton J. Sheen, *The World's First Love: Mary, Mother of God*, p. 211. Ignatius Press, 1996, San Francisco, CA.

October 7: Bl. Bartolo Longo, as quoted in Ann M. Brown, *Apostle of the Rosary: Blessed Bartolo Longo*, p. 53. New Hope Publications, 2004, New Hope, KY.

October 8: St. John Vianney, as quoted in *Thoughts of the Cure D'Ars*, compiled and arranged by W. M. B., p. 36. TAN Books, 1984, Charlotte, NC.

October 9: St. Augustine, as quoted in Fr. Paul Segneri, SJ, *The Devout Client of Mary: Instructed in the Motives and Means of Serving Her Well*, p. 32. Burns & Lambert, 1857, London.

October 10: *Catechism of the Catholic Church*, par. 1326.

October 11: Pope St. John XXIII, as quoted in Saint Joseph Adoration Monastery, *Manual for Eucharistic Adoration, The Poor Clares of Perpetual Adoration*, p. 113. TAN Books, 2016, Charlotte, NC.

October 12: St. Hilary, from the treatise On the Trinity, *The Liturgy of the Hours Vol. II*, p.780. Catholic Book Publishing Corp, 1976, New York.

October 13: St. Mary Euphrasia Pelletier, as quoted in *Magnificat*, Vol 14, No. 8, October 2012, p. 169.

October 14: Servant of God Lúcia Dos Santos, as quoted in Fr. Robert Fox, *The Intimate Life of Sister Lúcia* (2001), 316.

October 15: St. Teresa of Ávila, *The Way of Perfection*, p. 207. TAN Books, 2010, Charlotte, NC.

October 16: St. Margaret Mary Alacoque, as quoted in Servant of God Fr. Lukas Etlin, O.S.B., *Devotion To The Sacred Heart*, p. 25. TAN Books, 2012, Charlotte, NC.

October 17: St. Josemaria Escrivá, *Christ is Passing By*, p. 349. Scepter, 1973, New York, NY.

October 18: St. Luke 22: 15-20, *Divine Mercy Catholic Bible, Revised Standard Version, Second Catholic Edition*, revised according to Liturgiam Authenticam, p. 1381. Ascension Publishing, LCC, 2001, West Chester, PA.

October 19: St. Anthony Mary Claret, *Autobiography*, p. 272. Claretian Publications, 1976, Chicago, IL.

October 20: St. Peter of Alcantara, as quoted in Saint Joseph Adoration Monastery, *Manual for Eucharistic Adoration, The Poor Clares of Perpetual Adoration*, p. 117. TAN Books, 2016, Charlotte, NC.

October 21: St. Ambrose, as quoted in *The Catechism of the Council of Trent*, trans. John A. McHugh, O.P. and Charles J Callan, O.P., p. 253. TAN Books, 1982, Charlotte, NC.

October 22: Pope St. John Paul II, *Ecclesia de Eucharistia*, 1.

October 23: St. Hedwig, as quoted in Fr. Stefano M. Manelli, FI, *Jesus Our Eucharistic Love*, p. 97. Academy of the Immaculate, 2017, New Bedford, MA.

October 24: St. Gaudentius of Brescia, as quoted in Saint Joseph Adoration Monastery, *Manual for Eucharistic Adoration, The Poor Clares of Perpetual Adoration*, p. 106. TAN Books, 2016, Charlotte, NC.

October 25: St. Louis de Montfort, *Love of Eternal Wisdom*, p. 69. Montfort Publications, 1969, New York.

October 26: St. John Vianney, as quoted in *Thoughts of the Cure D'Ars*, compiled and arranged by W. M. B., p. 62. TAN Books, 1984, Charlotte, NC.

October 27: St. Ephrem as quoted in Pope St. John Paul II, *Ecclesia de Eucharistia*, 17.

October 28: Blessed Basil Moreau, *Basil Moreau: Essential Writings,* edited by Kevin Grove, CSC and Andrew Gawrych, CSC, p. 322. Christian Classics, 2014, Notre Dame, IN.

October 29: St. Peter Julian Eymard, *How To Get More Out Of Holy Communion*, ch. 6, 45. Sophia Institute Press, 2000, Manchester, NH.

October 30: Pope Benedict XVI, *God's Revolution, World Youth Day and Other Cologne Talks,* p. 60-61. Ignatius Press, 2006, San Francisco, CA.

October 31: St. Paul of the Cross, as quoted in Saint Joseph Adoration Monastery, *Manual for Eucharistic Adoration, The Poor Clares of Perpetual Adoration*, p. 109. TAN Books, 2016, Charlotte, NC.

November Image: *A Blessed Abbes Receiving the Host from the Hands of Christ*, Giovanni Battista Gaulli (1639–1709). Public Domain.

November 1: Pope St. Paul VI, *Solemni Hac Liturgia* (1968), no. 26.

November 2: St. Maximilian Kolbe, *The Writings of St. Maximilian Maria Kolbe: Volume II,* p. 1999. Nerbini International, 2016, Lugano.

November 3: Pope Leo XIII, *Mirae Caritatis On The Holy Eucharist*, 14.

November 4: St. Josemaría Escrivá, *Christ is Passing By,* p. 211, Scepter, 1973, New York, NY.

November 5: St. Peter Julian Eymard, as quoted in Raymond Moloney, SJ, *Our Splendid Eucharist, Reflections On Mass And Sacrament*, p. 140. Vertias Publications, 2003, Dublin, Ireland.

November 6: Bl. Columba Marmion, *Christ: The Ideal of the Priest*, p. 238. Ignatius Press, 2005, San Francisco, CA.

November 7: Servant of God Catherine Doherty, *Grace in Every Season: Through the Year with Catherine Doherty*, p. 339. Madonna House Publications, 2001, Ontario, Canada.

November 8: St. Joseph Sebastian Pelczar, "Thoughts of St. Joseph Sebastian Pelczar for Every Day of the Year," Sacred Heart Sisters, Nov. 16. www.sacredheart-sisters.org.

November 9: St. Teresa of Ávila, *The Way of Perfection*, p. 213. TAN Books, 2010, Charlotte, NC.

November 10: St. Andrew of Avellino, as quoted in Fr. Stefano M. Manelli, FI, *Jesus Our Eucharistic Love*, p. 25. Academy of the Immaculate, 2017, New Bedford, MA.

November 11: St. John Chrystostom as quoted in Pope St. Paul VI, *Mysterium Fidei*, n. 38.

November 12: St. Francisco Marto, as quoted in *Blessed Francisco of Fatima*, compiled by Msgr. Joseph A. Cirrincione, p. 25-26. TAN Books, 2016, Charlotte, NC.

November 13: St. Stanislaus Kostka, as quoted in Fr. Stefano M. Manelli, FI, *Jesus Our Eucharistic Love*, p. 75. Academy of the Immaculate, 2017, New Bedford, MA.

November 14: St. Faustina Kowalska, *Diary: Divine Mercy in My Soul*, no. 1487. Marian Press, 2005, Stockbridge, MA.

November 15: St. Albert the Great, as quoted in Dennis J. Billy, C.Ss.R., *The Mystery of the Eucharist, Voices from the Saints and Mystics*, p. 98. New City Press, 2014, Hyde Park, NY.

November 16: St. Gertrude, as quoted in St. Alphonsus Ligouri, *The Sermons of St. Alphonsus Liguori*, fourth edition, p. 238. TAN Books, 1982, Charlotte, NC.

November 17: St. Peter Julian Eymard, *Month of St. Joseph*, 2.

November 18: St. Francis De Sales, *Introduction to the Devout Life*, ch. 21, 68. Ignatius Press, San Francisco, CA and Lighthouse Catholic Media, 2015, DeKalb, IL.

November 19: St. Faustina Kowalska, *Diary: Divine Mercy in My Soul*, no. 1233. Marian Press, 2005, Stockbridge, MA.

November 20: Servant of God Frank Duff, *Legio Mariae: The Official Handbook of the Legion of Mary*, p. 137-138. De Montfort House, 1975, Dublin, Ireland.

November 21: Ven. Mary of Agreda, *The Mystical City of God. Vol. III*, trans. Rev. George J. Blatter, no. 489. TAN Books, 2006, Charlotte, NC.

November 22: St. Peter Julian Eymard, *How To Get More Out Of Holy Communion*, ch 7, 52. Sophia Institute Press, 2000, Manchester, NH.

November 23: Pope St. John Paul II, "Address to Young People of Bologna," September 27, 1997.

November 24: Pope Urban IV, encyclical letter *Transiturus*, as quoted in James T. O'Connor, *The Hidden Manna, A Theology of the Eucharist*, p. 304. Ignatius Press, 2005, San Francisco, CA.

November 25: Servant of God Frank Duff, *The Woman of Genesis*, 371. Praedicanda Publications, 1976, Dublin, Ireland.

November 26: Pope St. John Paul II, "Address to Italian Youth," November 8, 1978.

November 27: St. Augustine of Hippo, as quoted in *The Catechism of the Council of Trent*, trans. John A. McHugh, O.P. and Charles J Callan, O.P., p. 253. TAN Books, 1982, Charlotte, NC.

November 28: Bl. Anne Catherine Emmerich, *The Dolorous Passion of Our Lord Jesus Christ*, med. 8, 87. Burnes & Oates, 1928, London.

November 29: Bl. James Alberione, *Mary, Mother and Model: Feasts of Mary*, p. 118. Daughters of St. Paul, 1958, Boston, MA.

November 30: Bl. Columba Marmion, *Christ: The Ideal of the Priest*, p. 159. Ignatius Press, 2005, San Francisco, CA.

December Image: *The Virgin Adoring the Host*, Jean Auguste Dominique Ingres (1780-1867). Public Domain.

December 1: St. John Vianney, as quoted in *Thoughts of the Cure D'Ars*, compiled and arranged by W. M. B., p. 19. TAN Books, 1984, Charlotte, NC.

December 2: St. Francisco Marto, as quoted in *Blessed Francisco of Fatima*, compiled by Msgr. Joseph A. Cirrincione, p. 26. TAN Books, 2016, Charlotte, NC.

December 3: St. Ignatius of Loyola, as quoted in Raymond Moloney, SJ, *Our Splendid Eucharist, Reflections On Mass And Sacrament*, p. 136. Veritas Publications, 2003, Dublin, Ireland.

December 4: St. Matthew 28: 20, *Divine Mercy Catholic Bible, Revised Standard Version, Second Catholic Edition*, revised according to Liturgiam Authenticam, p. 1311. Ascension Publishing, LCC, 2001, West Chester, PA.

December 5: Bl. Gabriel Allegra, *Mary's Immaculate Heart: A Way to God*, p. 49. Franciscan Herald Press, 1985, Chicago, IL.

December 6: St. Irenaeus, as quoted in in Timothy P. O'Malley, *Real Presence. What Does It Mean and Why Does It Matter?* p. 46. Ave Maria Press, 2021, Norte Dame, IN.

December 7: St. Maximilian Kolbe, *The Writings of St. Maximilian Maria Kolbe: Volume II*, p. 1578, Nerbini International, 2016, Lugano.

December 8: St. Albert the Great, as quoted in Fr. Stefano M. Manelli, FI, *Jesus Our Eucharistic Love*, p. 108. Academy of the Immaculate, 2017, New Bedford, MA.

December 9: St. John Bosco, as quoted in Fr. Stefano M. Manelli, FI, *Jesus Our Eucharistic Love*, p. 91. Academy of the Immaculate, 2017, New Bedford, MA.

December 10: St. Peter Julian Eymard, *Our Lady of the Blessed Sacrament: Readings for the Month of May*, p. 68-69. Emmanuel Publications, 1930, Cleveland, OH.

December 11: St. Teresa of Calcutta, as quoted in Nancy C. Reeves and Bernadette Gasslein, *Gifts of the Eucharist, Stories to Transform and Inspire*, p. 89. Ave Maria Press, 2009, Norte Dame, IN.

December 12: Ven. Mary of Agreda, *The Mystical City of God, Vol. III*, trans. Rev. George J. Blatter, no. 491. TAN Books, 2006, Charlotte, NC.

December 13: St. Charles de Foucauld, as quoted in Dennis J. Billy, C.Ss.R., *The Mystery of the Eucharist, Voices from the Saints and Mystics*, p. 274. New City Press, 2014, Hyde Park, NY.

December 14: St. John of the Cross, as quoted in Dennis J. Billy, C.Ss.R., *The Mystery of the Eucharist, Voices from the Saints and Mystics*, p. 198-199. New City Press, 2014, Hyde Park, NY.

December 15: St. Thérèse of Lisieux, *The Story of a Soul*, trans. John Beevers, ch. 4, 43. Image, 2001, New York.

December 16: St. Peter Julian Eymard, *How To Get More Out Of Holy Communion*, ch. 10, 72. Sophia Institute Press, 2000, Manchester, NH.

December 17: Pope Leo XIII, *Mirae Caritatis (On The Holy Eucharist)*, 14.

December 18: St. Teresa of Ávila, *The Way of Perfection*, 208-209. TAN Books, 2010, Charlotte, NC.

December 19: St. Teresa Benedicta of the Cross, as quoted in Saint Joseph Adoration Monastery, *Manual for Eucharistic Adoration, The Poor Clares of Perpetual Adoration*, p. 107. TAN Books, 2016, Charlotte, NC.

December 20: St. John Vianney, as quoted in *Thoughts of the Cure D'Ars*, compiled and arranged by W. M. B., p. 18. TAN Books, 1984, Charlotte, NC.

December 21: Venerable Fulton J. Sheen, *The World's First Love: Mary, Mother of God*, p. 211. Ignatius Press, 1996, San Francisco, CA.

December 22: Venerable Joseph Mindszenty, *The Mother*, trans. Rev. Benedict P. Lenz, CSsR p. 42. Radio Replies Press, 1949, St. Paul, MN.

December 23: Bl. Mary Anne Blondin, as quoted in Nancy C. Reeves and Bernadette Gasslein, *Gifts of the Eucharist, Stories to Transform and Inspire*, p. 107. Ave Maria Press, 2009, Norte Dame, IN.

December 24: Venerable Fulton J. Sheen, *Three to Get Married*, p. 168. Scepter, 1951, Princeton, N.J.

December 25: St. Charles de Foucauld, as quoted in Dennis J. Billy, C.Ss.R., *The Mystery of the Eucharist, Voices from the Saints and Mystics*, p. 273-274. New City Press, 2014, Hyde Park, NY.

December 26: J.R.R. Tolkien, as quoted in James T. O'Connor, *The Hidden Manna, A Theology of the Eucharist*, p. 344. Ignatius Press, 2005, San Francisco, CA.

December 27: St John 6: 27, 47-48, 51, *Divine Mercy Catholic Bible*, Revised Standard Version, Second Catholic Edition, revised according to Liturgiam Authenticam, p. 1397. Ascension Publishing, LLC, 2001, West Chester, PA.

December 28: St. Faustina Kowalska, Diary: *Divine Mercy in My Soul*, no. 72. Marian Press, 2005, Stockbridge, MA.

December 29: St. Alphonsus Liguori, as quoted in Saint Joseph Adoration Monastery, *Manual for Eucharistic Adoration, The Poor Clares of Perpetual Adoration*, p. 111. TAN Books, 2016, Charlotte, NC.

December 30: Pope St. John Paul II, *Ecclesia de Eucharistia*, 9.

December 31: St. John Chrysostom, as quoted in *Thoughts of the Cure D'Ars*, compiled and arranged by W. M. B., p. 11. TAN Books, 1984, Charlotte, NC.

About the Author

Father Donald Calloway, MIC, a convert to Catholicism, is a member of the Congregation of the Marian Fathers of the Immaculate Conception. Before his conversion to Catholicism, he was a high school dropout who had been kicked out of a foreign country, institutionalized twice, and thrown in jail multiple times. After his radical conversion, he earned a B.A. in Philosophy and Theology from the Franciscan University of Steubenville, Ohio; M.Div. and S.T.B. degrees from the Dominican House of Studies in Washington, D.C.; and an S.T.L. in Mariology from the International Marian Research Institute in Dayton, Ohio. In addition to *Under the Mantle: Marian Thoughts from a 21st Century Priest* (Marian Press, 2013), he has written *No Turning Back: A Witness to Mercy* (Marian Press, 2010), a bestseller that recounts his conversion story. He also is the author of *Purest of All Lilies: The Virgin Mary in the Spirituality of St. Faustina* (Marian Press, 2008). He introduced and arranged *Marian Gems: Daily Wisdom on Our Lady* (Marian Press, 2014). He is the author of the international bestseller *Consecration to St. Joseph* (Marian Press, 2019) and co-author of *Consecration to St. Joseph for Children and Families* (Marian Press, 2022). Further, he has written academic articles and is the editor of *The Immaculate Conception in the Life of the Church* (Marian Press, 2004) and *The Virgin Mary and Theology of the Body* (Marian Press, 2005). Father Calloway is the Vicar Provincial and Vocation Director for the Mother of Mercy Province.

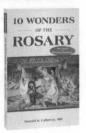
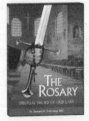

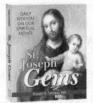

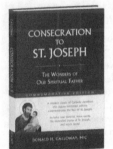
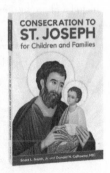

The Rosary is Mary's Prayer

THE HOLY ROSARY
You will treasure the meditations and colorful art accompanying every mystery of the Rosary in this booklet. Stephanie Wilcox-Hughes, 64 pages.
Y106-THRB
Spanish: Y106-THRS

PRAY THE ROSARY DAILY
Our most popular pamphlet includes Pope John Paul II's reflections on all four sets of mysteries of the Rosary. A complete guide to praying the Rosary.
Y106-PR2

MARIANS OF THE IMMACULATE CONCEPTION ROSARY GIFT SETS
These rosaries were designed exclusively for the Marians of the Immaculate Conception. They reflect our mission to spread the message of God's mercy through a devotion to Mary Immaculate. Each set comes enclosed in a matching gift box. **Y106-OMR3**

The Marian Fathers of Today and Tomorrow

What are you looking for in the priests of tomorrow?

- ☑ **Zeal for proclaiming the Gospel**
- ☑ **Faithfulness to the Pope and Church teaching**
- ☑ **Love of Mary Immaculate**
- ☑ **Love of the Holy Eucharist**
- ☑ **Concern for the souls in Purgatory**
- ☑ **Dedication to bringing God's mercy to all souls**

These are the top reasons why men pursuing a priestly vocation are attracted to the Congregation of Marian Fathers of the Immaculate Conception.

Please support the education of these future priests.
More than 30 Marian seminarians are counting on your gift.

Call: 1-800-462-7426
Online: Marian.org/helpseminarians

Join the
Association of Marian Helpers,
headquartered at the
National Shrine of The Divine Mercy,
and share in special blessings!

**An invitation from
Fr. Joseph, MIC, the director**

**Marian Helpers is an Association
of Christian faithful of the
Congregation of Marians of
the Immaculate Conception.**
By becoming a member, you share in
the spiritual benefits of the daily Masses,
prayers, and good works of the Marian
priests and brothers.

This is a special offer of grace given to you by the Church through
the Marian Fathers. Please consider this opportunity to share in
these blessings, along with others whom you would wish to join
into this spiritual communion.

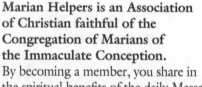

The Marian Fathers of the Immaculate Conception of the Blessed
Virgin Mary is a religious congregation of nearly 500 priests and
brothers around the world.

Call 1-800-462-7426 or visit Marian.org